THE TEACHER: DECISION MAKER AND CURRICULUM PLANNER

THE TEACHER
DECISION MAKER AND CURRICULUM PLANNER

Robert S. Harnack

Professor of Education
State University of New York
Buffalo, New York

INTERNATIONAL TEXTBOOK COMPANY
SCRANTON, PENNSYLVANIA

PREFACE

This book emphasizes the fact that teachers are professional workers who want to make choices about the best teaching-learning situation for pupils. To that end we have tried to examine certain ideas about teacher decision making.

Basically, we have tried to help teachers who are professional decision makers, teachers who aim in that direction, and teachers (pre-service and in-service) who have not accepted the point of view of professionalism with its corresponding obligations and responsibilities. But this material is also written for administrators, curriculum workers, supervisors, and laymen who have either inadvertently or purposely ignored the professionalism which already exists or who have chosen to ignore the fact that the profession of teaching has come of age.

Why was this thesis developed? Many answers to this question could be given, and in each case the answer probably would revolve about the growth of education as a profession. Specifically, theories of curriculum and instruction, the elaborate organizations and reorganizations of subject matter, and the growth of the body of professional knowledge, in itself the result of educational research, could be listed as possible reasons. Quite honestly, the basic purpose for developing this point of view arose because of the author's experiences in the field of curriculum planning. During the past fifteen years he has noticed two phenomena: Many knowledgeable, professional teachers became frustrated trying to make choices or decisions. At times they were frustrated by their own inabilities or lack of knowledge; at other times they were frustrated by an improper frame of reference within a school system. In like manner, there were times when these teachers felt that fascinating professional interest could not be pursued, pressing felt needs were not being met, and in general an administrative staff seemed more concerned about continuing in-service education (professional growth of the individual teacher) than utilizing already existing professional knowledge for the improvement of teaching-learning situations for pupils. In other words, the knowledgeable, conscientious teacher who tried to employ his education, his experiences, and his intelligence to solve educational problems or to choose a proper course of action was not allowed to participate in classroom decision making. We believe there is something wrong with such a milieu, frame of reference, or atmosphere. As an aside, we wonder what would happen in a hospital setting if a brain surgeon made specific decisions which would then be countermanded by the superintendent of the hospital.

To the imaginative and driving worker in education the challenge to improve instruction is an exciting challenge. His exuberant, active disposition toward decision making and curriculum planning has led him to experimentation and evidence. He welcomes instructional problems, and his solutions are based on curriculum-planning methods and theories which have appeared in many excellent books and articles. For him the organized and systematic concepts of planning have evolved into a workable structure which he employs continuously.

Today, the bulk of educational workers seek to improve instruction because they are no longer satisfied with weird procedures sometimes labeled the "rest-room theory of curriculum planning." This writer sincerely feels that soon the breakthrough will be a rout, and systematic curriculum planning activities will be common in most local schools. To that end the local school administrative staff and the teachers, as well as pupils and laymen, will organize for the job.

We feel that teacher decision making and curriculum planning is "in the air." Systematic improvement of instruction "is a must." The professional staff wants to "get at it."

These trite expressions are trying to say that the professional workers in education are thinking seriously about the educational program, and they are concerned with making an organized attempt to work out the curriculum problems that confront them.

Today the administrator's desk is crowded with a jumble of curricular problems which he and his staff have identified and which they want to attack. Today the teaching staff wants to be professional and scientific in their outlook. Instructional objectives, subject matter, and classroom methods and materials, as well as evaluating devices, are concepts and tools to be used with the same delicate understanding that the surgeon employs when he uses his instruments in the operating room. Today, as always, the community people are waiting patiently for their "average" school to provide the best educational program available for their children. These same community people are honestly saying to the professional staff, "Tell us how we can help." The bald, harsh, adverse criticisms from certain laymen have been replaced by the conviction that serious investigation of the school's program is underway, and that the professional staff directing this investigation will not lose sight of the firm belief that public education depends on the understanding that the public has of its schools.

For the teacher who is not professional, perhaps the chapters that follow will help him to define his task. For administrators, curriculum workers, laymen, and others who have not considered the teacher a professional worker, perhaps this book will help them to help teachers.

Specifically, this book begins by quoting John Dewey's speech to the Parents' Association of the University Elementary School in Chicago in February, 1899. In that speech Dewey discusses certain curricular and administrative aspects of the laboratory school. Our major purpose for quoting this entire speech was twofold: It emphasizes the questions and problems (four in number) which served as a frame of reference for Dewey's staff in planning the curricular experiences for the boys and girls. Second, it emphasizes that within this frame of reference the teachers themselves had to be the decision makers who made the educational choices. Continuing in this vein, the second chapter points out that the profession of education has improved during the past sixty-five years, and happenings in professional education since 1957 have given an added push to teacher decision making. In other words we have reached the point at which teachers are forced to make choices in their everyday professional activities. However, a basic concern arises: Are there global questions which teaching staffs must try to answer because the lack of answers may decrease their ability to make choices on the classroom level of operation?

Chapter 3 describes the frame of reference—curriculum planning—which must serve as the milieu in which the professional teacher thrives and grows. Chapters 4 and 5 discuss the needs and responsibilities of teachers who have lived in this atmosphere. Chapter 6 is written for all personnel who support the teacher in his daily activity. This chapter points out that the teacher cannot stand alone as he tries to be professional. He cannot operate without the help of the supportive services around him. However, when supportive personnel do not consider the teacher a professional worker, they do not provide an atmosphere or a frame of reference which allows for teacher decision making or for teacher curriculum planning. Therefore, we have tried to develop for supportive personnel certain guidelines which are directly related to professional teacher decision making or which might help create a climate conducive to allowing the teacher to practice his profession. Chapter 7 strongly emphasizes that we can never turn our backs on a philosophy which prizes valuing, an intelligent process for determining the worth of alternatives.

ROBERT S. HARNACK

Buffalo, New York
January, 1968

CONTENTS

CHAPTER ONE

A TALK BY JOHN DEWEY

Perhaps some readers might consider that beginning a book by quoting an entire chapter from another book is unusual. In a way, it is. However, for years we have been thoughtfully impressed with the last chapter of John Dewey's *School and Society*.[1] It not only is a delightful talk to the Parents' Association of the University Elementary School; it also contains two elements that are basic to this book.

First, Dewey emphasizes that he and the staff did not have any "ready-made . . . principles"[2] regarding the best education for youth. Instead, he says, they started by looking at the problems and questions that they felt needed answers. Four such questions and problems are listed and discussed in Dewey's talk. For our purposes, the questions and problems posed are highly appropriate today. These questions, and others, serve curriculum planners as a basis for decision making. Seeking the answers to these questions and problems is the gist of the activity of professional educators. Finding appropriate answers to questions and problems about the improvement of instruction is the purpose of curriculum planning.

Second, Dewey emphasizes that he and the staff, together, sought the answers and solutions. He states, quite clearly, that he is not the author of these answers. Instead he says that he

---

[1] John Dewey, *The School and Society* (New York: McClure, Phillips and Company, 1900), pp. 113–29.
[2] *Ibid.*, pp. 115–16.

1

and the teaching staff were involved in choosing and making decisions about the education of children. Still more important for our purpose, Dewey considered his teaching staff to be professional decision makers who had the right and obligation to make choices regarding an appropriate course of action. His teachers were not merely consulted; they made the decisions. Teacher involvement in curriculum planning was not for purposes of professional growth while in service; teacher involvement served to plan for the improvement of the instructional program. Dewey implies that his teaching staff was professional, that the responsibility for choosing the best course of action belonged to the teachers, and (quite matter of factly) that when answers were supplied they came from the teaching staff.

John Dewey had respect for his viable staff. This respect and a reliance on a philosophy of pragmatism caused them to seek out both significant questions and careful answers. Near the end of his talk, which we are about to quote in full length, John Dewey says: "The presence of an organized corps of instructors demonstrates that thoroughly educated teachers are ready to bring to elementary education the same resources of training, knowledge, and skill that have long been at the command of higher education."[3]

IV
THREE YEARS OF THE UNIVERSITY
ELEMENTARY SCHOOL*

The school was started the first week in January, three years ago. I shall try this afternoon to give a brief statement of the ideas and problems that were in mind when the experiment was started, and a sketch of the development of the work since that time. We began in a small house in Fifty-seventh Street, with fifteen children. We found ourselves the next year with twenty-five children in Kimbark Avenue, and then moved in January to Rosalie Court, the larger quarters enabling us to take forty children. The next year the numbers increased to sixty, the school remaining at Rosalie Court. This year we have had ninety-

---

[3] *Ibid.*, p. 129.
* Stenographic report of a talk by John Dewey at a meeting of the Parents' Association of the University Elementary School, February, 1899; somewhat revised.

five on the roll at one time, and are located at 5412 Ellis Avenue, where we hope to stay till we have a building and grounds of our own.

The children during the first year of the school were between the ages of six and nine. Now their ages range between four and thirteen—the members of the oldest group being in their thirteenth year. This is the first year that we have children under six, and this has been made possible through the liberality of friends in Honolulu, H.I., who are building up there a memorial kindergarten along the same lines.

The expenses of the school during the first year, of two terms only, were between $1,300 and $1,400. The expenses this year will be about $12,000. Of this amount $5,500 will come from tuitions; $5,000 has been given by friends interested in the school, and there remains about $1,500 yet to be raised for the conduct of the school. This is an indication of the increase of expenses. The average expense per pupil is about the same since the start, i.e., $120 per child per school year. Relatively speaking, this year the expenses of the school took something of a jump, through the expense of moving to a new building, and the repairs and changes there necessary. An increase in the staff of teachers has also enlarged the work as well as the debits of the school. Next year (1899–1900) we hope to have about 120 children, and apparently the expenses will be about $2,500 more than this. Of this amount $2,000 will be met by the increase in tuition from the pupils. The cost of a child to the school, $120 a year, is precisely the tuition charged by the University for students and is double the average tuition charged by the school. But it is not expected that the University tuition will come anywhere near meeting the expense involved there. One reason for not increasing the tuition here, even if it were advisable for other reasons, is that it is well to emphasize, from an educational point of view, that elementary as well as advanced education requires endowment. There is every reason why money should be spent freely for the organization and maintenance of foundation work in education as well as for the later stages.

The elementary school has had from the outset two sides: one, the obvious one of instruction of the children who have been intrusted to it; the other, relationship to the University, since the school is under the charge, and forms a part of the pedagogical work of the University.

When the school was started, there were certain ideas in mind—perhaps it would be better to say questions and problems; certain points which it seemed worth while to test. If you will permit one personal word, I should like to say that it is sometimes thought that the school started out with a number of ready-made principles and ideas which were to be put into practice at once. It has been popularly assumed that I am the author of these ready-made ideas and principles which were to go into execution. I take this opportunity to say that the educational conduct of the school, as well as its administration, the selection of subject-matter, and the working out of the course of study, as well as actual instruction of children, have been almost entirely in the hands of the teachers of the school; and that there has been a gradual development of the educational principles and methods involved, not a fixed equipment. The teachers started with question marks, rather than with fixed rules, and if any answers have been reached, it is the teachers in the school who have supplied them. We started upon the whole with four such questions, or problems:

1. What can be done, and how can it be done, to bring the school into closer relation with the home and neighborhood life —instead of having the school a place where the child comes solely to learn certain lessons? What can be done to break down the barriers which have unfortunately come to separate the school life from the rest of the everyday life of the child? This does not mean, as it is sometimes, perhaps, interpreted to mean, that the child should simply take up in the school things already experienced at home and study them, but that, so far as possible, the child shall have the same attitude and point of view in the school as in the home; that he shall find the same interest in going to school, and in there doing things worth doing for their own sake, that he finds in the plays and occupations which busy him in his home and neighborhood life. It means, again, that the motives which keep the child at work and growing at home shall be used in the school, so that he shall not have to acquire another set of principles of actions belonging only to the school—separate from those of the home. It is a question of the unity of the child's experience, of its actuating motives and aims, not of amusing or even interesting the child.

2. What can be done in the way of introducing subject-matter in history and science and art, that shall have a positive value and real significance in the child's own life; that shall represent, even to the youngest children, something worthy of attainment in skill or knowledge; as much so to the little pupil as are the studies of the high-school or college student to him? You know what the traditional curriculum of the first few years is, even though many modifications have been made. Some statistics have been collected showing that 75 or 80 per cent of the first three years of a child in school are spent upon the form—not the substance—of learning, the mastering of the symbols of reading, writing, and arithmetic. There is not much positive nutriment in this. Its purpose is important—is necessary—but it does

not represent the same kind of increase in a child's intellectual and moral experience that is represented by positive truth of history and nature, or by added insight into reality and beauty. One thing, then, we wanted to find out is how much can be given a child that is really worth his while to get, in knowledge of the world about him, of the forces in the world, of historical and social growth, and in capacity to express himself in a variety of artistic forms. From the strictly educational side this has been the chief problem of the school. It is along this line that we hope to make our chief contribution to education in general; we hope, that is, to work out and publish a positive body of subject-matter which may be generally available.

3. How can instruction in these formal, symbolic branches —the mastering of the ability to read, write, and use figures intelligently—be carried on with everyday experience and occupation as their background and in definite relations to other studies of more inherent content, and be carried on in such a way that the child shall feel their necessity through their connection with subjects which appeal to him on their own account? If this can be accomplished, he will have a vital motive for getting the technical capacity. It is not meant, as has been sometimes jocosely stated, that the child learn to bake and sew at school, and to read, write, and figure at home. It is intended that these formal subjects shall not be presented in such large doses at first as to be the exclusive objects of attention, and that the child shall be led by that which he is doing to feel the need for acquiring skill in the use of symbols and the immediate power they give. In any school, if the child realizes the motive for the use and application of number and language he has taken the longest step toward securing the power; and he can realize the motive only as he has some particular—not some general and remote—use for the symbols.

4. Individual attention. This is secured by small groupings— eight or ten in a class—and a large number of teachers supervising systematically the intellectual needs and attainments and physical well-being and growth of the child. To secure this we have now 135 hours of instructors' time per week, that is, the time of nine teachers for three hours per day, or one teacher per group. It requires but a few words to make this statement about attention to individual powers and needs, and yet the whole of the school's aims and methods, moral, physical, intellectual, are bound up in it.

I think these four points present a fair statement of what we have set out to discover. The school is often called an experimental school, and in one sense that is the proper name. I do not like to use it too much, for fear parents will think we are experimenting upon the children, and that they naturally object to. But it is an experimental school—at least I hope so—with reference to education and educational problems. We have attempted to find out by trying, by doing—not alone by discussion and theorizing—*whether* these problems may be worked out, and *how* they may be worked out.

Next a few words about the means that have been used in the school in order to test these four questions, and to supply their answers, and first as to the place given to hand-work of different kinds in the school. There are three main lines regularly pursued: (a) the shop work with wood and tools, (b) cooking work, and (c) work with textiles—sewing and weaving. Of course, there is other hand-work in connection with science, as science is largely of an experimental nature. It is a fact that may not have come to your attention that a large part of the best and most advanced scientific work involves a great deal of manual skill, the training of the hand and eye. It is impossible for one to be a first-class worker in science without this training in manipulation, and in handling apparatus and materials. In connection with the history work, especially with the younger children, hand-work is brought in in the way of making implements, weapons, tools, etc. Of course, the art work is another side—drawing, painting, and modeling. Logically, perhaps, the gymnasium work does not come in here, but as a means of developing moral and intellectual control through the medium of the body it certainly does. The children have one-half hour per day of this form of physical exercise. Along this line we have found that hand-work, in large variety and amount, is the most easy and natural method of keeping up the same attitude of the child in and out of the school. The child gets the largest part of his acquisitions through his bodily activities, until he learns to work systematically with the intellect. That is the purpose of this work in the school, to direct these activities, to systematize and organize them, so that they shall not be as haphazard and as wandering as they are outside of school. The problem of making these forms of practical activity work continuously and definitely together, leading from one factor of skill to another, from one intellectual difficulty to another, has been one of the most difficult, and at the same time one in which we have been most successful. The various kinds of work, carpentry, cooking, sewing, and weaving, are selected as involving different kinds of skill, and demanding different types of intellectual attitude on the part of the child, and because they represent some of the most important activities of the everyday outside world: the question of living under shelter, of daily food and clothing, of the home, of personal movement and exchange of goods. He gets also the training of sense organs, of touch, of sight, and the ability to coördinate eye and hand. He gets healthy exercise; for the child demands a much larger amount of physical activity than the formal program of the ordinary school permits. There is also a continual appeal to memory, to judgment, in adapting ends to means, a training in habits of order, industry, and neatness in the care of the tools and utensils, and in doing things in a systematic, instead of a haphazard, way. Then, again, these practical occupations make a background, especially in the earlier groups, for the later studies. The children get a good deal of chemistry in connection with cooking, of number work and geometrical principles in carpentry, and a good deal of geography in connection with their theoretical work in weaving and sewing. History also comes in with the origin and growth of various inventions, and their effects upon social life and political organization.

Perhaps more attention, upon the whole, has been given to our second point, that of positive subject-matter, than to any one other thing. On the history side the curriculum is now fairly well worked out. The younger children begin with the home and occupations of the home. In the sixth year the intention is that the children should study occupations outside the home, the larger social industries—farming, mining, lumber, etc.—that they may see the complex and various social industries on which life depends, while incidentally they investigate the use of the various materials—woods, metals, and the processes applied— thus getting a beginning of scientific study. The next year is given to the historical development of industry and invention— starting with man as a savage and carrying him through the typical phases of his progress upward, until the iron age is reached and man begins to enter upon a civilized career. The object of the study of primitive life is not to keep the child interested in lower and relatively savage stages, but to show him the steps of progress and development, especially along the line of invention, by which man was led into civilization. There is a certain nearness, after all, in the child to primitive forms of life. They are much more simple than existing institutions. By throwing the emphasis upon the progress of man, and upon the way advance has been made, we hope to avoid the objections that hold against paying too much attention to the crudities and distracting excitements of savage life.

The next two or three years, i.e., the fourth and fifth grades, and perhaps the sixth, will be devoted to American history. It is then that history, properly speaking, begins, as the study of primitive life can hardly be so called.

Then comes Greek history and Roman, in the regular chronological order, each year having its own work planned with reference to what has come before and after.

The science work was more difficult to arrange and systematize, because there was so little to follow—so little that has been already done in an organized way. We are now at work upon a program* and I shall not speak in detail about it. The first two or three years cultivate the children's powers of observation, lead them to sympathetic interest in the habits of plants and animals, and to look at things with reference to their uses. Then the center of the work becomes geographical—the study of the earth, as the most central thing. From this almost all the work grows out, and to it the work goes back. Another standpoint in the science work is that of the application of natural forces to the service of man through machines. Last year a good deal of work was done in electricity (and will be repeated this year), based on the telegraph and telephone—taking up the things that can easily be grasped.

In mechanics they have studied locks and clocks with reference to the adaptation of the various parts of the machinery. All this work makes a most excellent basis for more formal physics later on. Cooking gives opportunity for getting a great many ideas of heat and water, and of their effects. The scientific work taken up in the school differs mainly from that of other schools in having the experimental part—physics and chemistry—emphasized, and is not confined simply to nature study—the study of plants and animals. Not that the latter is less valuable, but that we find it possible to introduce the physical aspects from the first.

If I do not spend a large amount of time in speaking of the music and art work, it is not because they are not considered valuable and important—certainly as much so as any other work done in the school, not only in the development of the child's moral and æsthetic nature, but also from a strictly intellectual point of view. I know of no work in the school that better develops the power of attention, the habit of observation and of consecutiveness, of seeing parts in relation to a whole.

I shall now say a few words about the administrative side of the school. At the outset we mixed up the children of different ages and attainments as much as possible, believing there were mental advantages in the give-and-take thus secured, as well as the moral advantages in having the older assume certain responsibilities in the care of the younger. As the school grew, it became necessary to abandon the method, and to group the children with reference to their common capacities. These groupings, however, are based, not on ability to read and write, but upon similarity of mental attitude and interest, and upon gen-

---

* This year's program is published in the *Elementary School Record*. Address The University of Chicago Press for particulars.

eral intellectual capacity and mental alertness. There are ways in which we are still trying to carry out the idea of mixing up the children, that we may not build the rigid step ladder system of the "graded" school. One step in this direction is having the children move about and come in contact with different teachers. While there are difficulties and evils connected with this, I think one of the most useful things in the school is that children come into intimate relation with a number of different personalities. The children also meet in general assemblies— for singing, and for the report of the whole school work as read by members of the different groups. The older children are also given a half hour a week in which to join some of the younger groups, and, if possible, as in hand work, enter into the work of the younger children. In various ways we are attempting to keep a family spirit throughout the school, and not the feeling of isolated classes and grades.

The organization of the teaching force has gradually become departmental, as the needs of the work have indicated its chief branches. So we now have recognized divisions of Science, History, Domestic or Household Arts, Manual Training in the limited sense (wood and metals), Music, Art (that is, drawing, water colors, clay modeling, etc.), and Gymnasium. As the work goes on into the secondary period, the languages and mathematics will also of necessity assume a more differentiated and distinct position. As it is sometimes said that correlated or thoroughly harmonized work cannot be secured upon this basis, I am happy to say that our experience shows positively that there are no intrinsic difficulties. Through common devotion to the best development of the child, through common loyalty to the main aims and methods of the school, our teachers have demonstrated that in education, as in business, the best organization is secured through proper regard for natural divisions of labor, interest, and training. The child secures the advantage in discipline and knowledge of contact with experts in each line, while the individual teachers serve the common thought in diverse ways, thus multiplying and re-inforcing it.

Upon the moral side, that of so-called discipline and order, where the work of the University Elementary School has perhaps suffered most from misunderstanding and misrepresentation, I shall say only that our ideal has been, and continues to be, that of the best form of family life, rather than that of a rigid graded school. In the latter, the large number of children under the care of a single teacher, and the very limited number of modes of activity open to the pupils, have made necessary certain fixed and somewhat external forms of "keeping order." It would be very stupid to copy these, under the changed conditions of our school, its small groups permitting and requiring the most intimate personal acquaintance of child and teacher, and its great variety of forms of work, with their differing adaptations to the needs of different children. If we have permitted to our children more than the usual amount of freedom, it has not been in order to relax or decrease real discipline, but because under our particular conditions larger and less artificial responsibilities could thus be required of the children, and their entire development of body and spirit be more harmonious and complete. And I am confident that the parents who have intrusted their children to us for any length of time will agree in saying that, while the children like, or love, to come to school, yet work, and not amusement, has been the spirit and teaching of the school; and that this freedom has been granted under such conditions of intelligent and sympathetic oversight as to be a means of upbuilding and strengthening character.

At the end of three years, then, we are not afraid to say that some of our original questions have secured affirmative answers. The increase of our children from fifteen to almost one hundred, along with a practical doubling of fees, has shown that parents are ready for a form of education that makes individual growth its sole controlling aim. The presence of an organized corps of instructors demonstrates that thoroughly educated teachers are ready to bring to elementary education the same resources of training, knowledge, and skill that have long been at the command of higher education. The everyday work of the school shows that children can live in school as out of it, and yet grow daily in wisdom, kindness, and the spirit of obedience —that learning may, even with little children, lay hold upon the substance of truth that nourishes the spirit, and yet the forms of knowledge be observed and cultivated; and that growth may be genuine and thorough, and yet a delight.

CHAPTER TWO

THE TEACHER: DECISION MAKER

In February, 1899, when John Dewey spoke to the Parents' Association of the University Elementary School in Chicago he emphasized, quite succinctly, that in this experimental school, "if any answers have been reached, it is the teachers in the school who have supplied them." Today, there are *many* more questions about the education of children which concern the staff and which require total staff thinking for answers. Our purpose is to review some of these pertinent questions as they relate to the temporary education scene and especially as they emphasize and re-emphasize the active role of teachers in curriculum planning.

Today, professionally speaking, the extreme wealth of theoretical background and factual evidence in professional education indicates the obvious: teachers have a firmer base upon which to make choices for a learner. In fact, with the steady growth of school innovations (basically related to professional knowledge), there is a thick cluster of knowledges that is known by the teacher about teaching-learning situations. Therefore, the teacher—especially the teacher—must help to make intelligent decisions related to curriculum planning. His decisions, in the main, will revolve about the screening and selection of specific instructional objectives, the identification of centers of interest, the identification and organization of subject matter, the selection of instructional techniques and materials, and the selection of measuring devices to help him realize whether or not the objectives were accomplished. Be-

11

yond such individual decision making for students, the teacher, or his representative, will also be involved, from time to time, in decision making of greater scope in order that classroom decision making may be facilitated.[1]

THE NECESSITY FOR TEACHER DECISION MAKING

Cooperative and individual teacher decision making in today's school is a necessary staff activity. Multiple courses of action make intelligent choosing a professional way of life. The objectives of public education, alone, are so diversified and so large in number that we seek ways to classify them.[2] The explosion and reorganization of complex subject matter reduces a simple content outline for the classroom to an archaic appendage. Theories regarding how such subject matter might be organized are numerous and detailed in their explanations. The school library can no longer contain the wealth of instructional materials from which a teacher must choose. The "passing of the recitation" has become a reality, and the teacher today chooses to employ large group, small group, or individual techniques for working with students. Measuring devices are rapidly being developed which correspond to the diverse objectives. Information about the learner, his reading level, his interests, and his needs, emphasizes, in bold type, that the teacher no longer plows a single row for purposes of planting educational knowledge. Literally, decisions have to be made. A single, arbitrary, restricting, pattern of action still exists, but it is no longer rational.

---

[1] Virgil E. Herrick probably gave more thought than any other educator to the area of teacher decision making. Many of his thoughts have been gathered in the following book: *Strategies of Curriculum Development, Selected Writings of the late Virgil E. Herrick*, ed. James B. Macdonald, Dan W. Anderson, and Frank B. May (Columbus, Ohio: Charles E. Merrill Books, Inc., 1965).

[2] *Taxonomy of Educational Objectives, The Classification of Educational Goals, Handbook I: Cognitive Domain*, ed. Benjamin S. Bloom (New York: David McKay Company, Inc., 1956); and David R. Krathwohl, Benjamin S. Bloom, and Bertram B. Masia, *Taxonomy of Educational Objectives, the Classification of Education Goals, Handbook II: Affective Domain* (New York: David McKay Company, Inc., 1956).

In regard to contemporary education, a brief analysis of four areas will show the revolutionary changes which are taking place in professional education and which will require teacher decision making on the cooperative level and on the individual level. These areas are: (1) individualization of instruction, (2) staff utilization, (3) reorganization of subject-matter areas, and (4) the development of instructional materials.

Individualization of Instruction

When one considers the necessity for teacher decision making in today's education, the belief in individualization of instruction stands out clearly as an overwhelming reason for emphasizing this point. The excellent yearbooks, pamphlets, and articles about this subject indicate the genuine professional concern of individuals and groups for making this area a reality, once and for all. The following authors probably say it best when they write:

> If nurturing individuality were the same as what is commonly meant by 'taking care of individual differences,' the problem would be relatively simple. But there is a world of difference between the two phrases—even though providing for individual differences is a very important matter in its own right. 'Individuality' has to do with the whole person; it is a matter of personality and character, or integration and integrity, of ego strength and moral fiber. 'Individual differences,' at least as the words are most often used, has to do with ranges of achievement, competence, and interest. . . .

> But the truth goes deeper; the very conception of 'individual differences' is too narrow and limiting for our purposes. We say this with no implication of belittlement. The progressive recognition of the magnitude of such differences has made a huge contribution to education, and we salute all teachers who have struggled with almost inconceivable varieties and ranges of difference and have managed to make adjustments to many levels. The struggle must go on. Yet the fact remains that almost invariably the mention of individual differences connotes more nostalgia for some imagined norm than joy at the discovery of uniqueness. Individuality is something far beyond the sum of all a child's individual differences. And thoughtful provision for the full flowering of each individual requires conceptions of a higher order. The idea of sending a man to the moon and bringing him back safe and sound is a puny concept and a simple undertaking compared to the belief that every man is

unique and important and that education can be designed and executed so that every man can achieve his full potential.' [Finis E. Engleman, Shirley Cooper, and William J. Ellena, *Vignettes on the Theory and Practices of School Administration* (New York: Macmillan Co., 1963), p. 220].[3]

When a group of teachers, or an individual teacher, is vitally concerned with the identification of specific instructional objectives for a single learner—not a group—as well as being vitally concerned with the subject matter which corresponds to those objectives and to the individual differences of that learner from other learners, the group, or teacher, generates the ultimate in professional teacher decision making. Basically, this concept overrides the simple classroom objectives, the single class content outline, the narrow syllabus issued by a state department, or a curriculum guide issued by a school system to cover a single grade level or a departmental area. These restrictive items are passé. They are no longer realistic for purposes of achieving individualization of instruction. In like manner, they are no longer realistic for the professional teacher decision maker. Today's teacher, concerned with the contemporary education scene, no longer accepts such restrictive thinking. He wants to move, within the expansive framework of curriculum planning, toward the ultimate of teacher decision making—the development of unique teaching-learning situations for individual pupils.

Staff Utilization

Consider such items as team teaching, modular scheduling, teacher's assistants, and large group, small group, and independent supervised study for learners. The ultimate use of these activities cannot be achieved without cooperative and individual teacher decision making. Any teacher who has been involved in the various types of staff utilization in modern, innovating schools will rapidly list the numerous planning sessions, the difficult choices to be made, and the on-the-spot decisions which permeated his workaday world in education.

---

[3] American Association of School Administrators, Association for Supervision and Curriculum Development, National Association of Secondary School Principals, and NEA Department of Rural Education, *A Climate for Individuality* (Washington, D.C.: The Associations, 1965), pp. 10–12.

Any principal, supervisor, or curriculum worker who has reflected on the change of operation in his school as a result of different forms of staff utilization is quick to emphasize how, suddenly, under the new staff utilization format, he became an important catalyst in helping teachers arrive at decisions. The point is obvious: the numerous changes in staff utilization in elementary and secondary education have necessitated new decisions and teacher-made decisions.

Organizing Subject Matter

Choosing and organizing subject matter for the benefit of the learner has been discussed by many authors during recent times and no doubt will continue to be a focal point for serious reflection.[4] Regardless of the fine writings by contemporary authors, the most exacting statement was concisely written by John Dewey in the chapter "The Nature of Subject Matter" in his book *Democracy in Education*. In order to emphasize this point and in order to sum up the prolific writings about this area, perhaps this single quote by Dewey will suffice.

From the standpoint of the educator, in other words, the various studies represent working resources, available capital. Their remoteness from the experience of the young is not, however, seeming; it is real. The subject matter of the learner is not, therefore, it cannot be, identical with the formulated, the crystallized, and systematized subject matter of the adult; the material as found in books and in works of art, etc. The latter represents the possibilities of the former; not its existing state. It enters directly into the activities of the expert and the educator, not into that of the beginner, the learner. Failure to bear in mind the difference in subject matter from the respective standpoints of teacher and student is responsible for most of the mistakes made in the use of tests and other expressions of pre-existent knowledge.[5]

---

[4] Association for Supervision and Curriculum Development, *New Curriculum Developments*, ed. Glenys G. Unruh (Washington, D.C.: The Association, 1965); Jerome S. Bruner, *The Process of Education* (Cambridge, Mass.: Harvard University Press, 1961); and *The Structure of Knowledge and the Curriculum*, eds. G. W. Ford and Lawrence Pugno (Chicago: Rand McNally and Co., 1964). Because many authors, commissions, and associations have written about this area, many other publications could have been listed.

[5] John Dewey, *Democracy and Education* (New York: The Macmillan Co., 1916), pp. 214–15.

For purposes of our thesis, the role of the teacher in choosing and organizing subject matter for learners cannot be ignored any longer. It cannot be ignored because the overwhelming amount of different suggestions made by national committees, commissions, and textbook writers have opened so many avenues to possible organization of subject-matter areas that teacher decision making is actually a necessity. The advent of such teacher decision making was not sudden. Historically, decision making related to content in the classroom could probably be correlated with the higher education upgrading of public school teachers. Such decision making was certainly forced upon teachers with the advent of the "source unit" concept developed in the late 30's.[6] In like manner, since 1957, the growth of subject-matter commissions in such areas as mathematics, science, and English have presented the public school teachers with dozens of alternatives related to the choosing of subject-matter content outlines for class groups or for individual learners. In other words, an abundance of suggestions for the organization of subject-matter content outlines for learners forces the contemporary teacher to take a stand. He must choose from the suggestions of the experts. He must make a decision for the benefit of his learners. He cannot ignore the responsibility to adopt and to adapt suggestions for the reorganization of subject matter in keeping with his chosen specific instructional objectives and the characteristics of the learner in his classroom.

The Growth of Instructional Materials

Anyone, layman or professional, who has recently visited an instructional materials center located in a university or in a public school system would be appalled at the large amounts of instructional materials available to the teacher in any grade level or subject-matter area. In like manner, any teacher who has studied the list of instructional materials in a single resource unit related to a specific topic would be pleased to dis-

---

[6] Mildred L. Biddick, *The Preparation and Use of Source Units* (New York: Progressive Education Association, n.d.), (mimeographed); and Lavone A. Hanna, "Source Units," *Stanford Social Education Investigation*, I (September 1939), (mimeographed).

cover the varied materials at his disposal. In a specific resource unit the teacher would find a reservoir of books and pamphlets, as well as films, filmstrips, models, and realia.[7] To the professional teacher, this is a "mouth watering" surprise. He knows that, in relation to the specific instructional objectives he wishes to accomplish and in relation to the specific characteristics of his learners, he will be able to choose (make decisions related to) instructional materials for the common group (large group), small group, and individuals studying with him. Again, whether the teacher wants to or not, he is forced to make decisions.

When the above four items are woven together, which they must be in the practical situation, they write a persistent message which reads: "Teachers need to make choices." This is a fascinating statement. This statement has caused many practicing professionals in administration, curriculum planning, supervision, and teaching to ponder the ramifications. For example, if a teacher should make decisions in education, what are the screens of selection he would use as a basis for such decision making? Further, if the teacher does make professional teaching-learning decisions, what prior choices, not within the scope of classroom teaching, may constrict his decision making on the classroom level? Also, should groups of teachers, working together, spell out the guidelines whereby cooperative action assures the further development of decision making on a grade level, departmental level, and systemwide level? When a teacher seeks desperately to improve his professional abilities as a decision maker, what are his needs, interests, wants, and desires? Also, when a teacher seeks to improve his ability as a decision maker, to what obligations and responsibilities must he subscribe? Finally, what are the duties of the supportive services in a school system where personnel are concerned with aiding teachers?

---

[7] The fantastic jumble of instructional materials has caused individuals and groups to try to define a system of classifying and arranging instructional materials. See, for example: Patrick Meredith, "Toward a Taxonomy of Educational Media," *AV Communication Review,* XIII (Winter 1965), 374–84.

For the remainder of this chapter, we would like to consider the first two questions posed. What are the curricular screens of selection for decision making, and are their prior decisions made on a level other than classroom teaching which constrict the improvement of classroom decision making?

SCREENS OF SELECTION

Forcing a teacher to make choices forces a teacher to consider the intellectual means related to choosing. A teacher seeking an action pattern related to an aim or some problematic teaching-learning situation is inevitably forced to consider "the best road to take." The teacher who must choose cannot help but explore what A. S. Barr called the "limiting and facilitating aspects of the immediate situation." He is forced to appraise the separate factors—screens of selection—which constitute the means he will use. For example, the person who wants to travel from Boston to Washington, D.C. must decide what is the best mode of transportation. He could walk, or he could travel via automobile, airplane, train, or ship for that matter. In any case, he has various aspects to consider. Walking would make the trip very time consuming, indeed! Flying in an airplane may be frightening. Driving an automobile would provide him with transportation at his destination. In like manner, the teacher who wants to make decisions about a teaching-learning situation would also consider certain factors automatically. For example, are the children first graders or eleventh graders? Do they know how to read? If they know how to read, then printed matter could be used. But should the printed matter be in the form of a single textbook, supplementary books, programmed instruction, or all three? Is it feasible to take a field trip? Perhaps a field trip will interfere with a test scheduled for another departmental area. Is there a relationship between learning theory and the organization of the subject matter for the teaching-learning situation?

At times, the factors, or screens, that influence a teacher's decisions are simple; at other times, they are highly complex. Whether or not a child can read certainly seems to be a simple factor that influences a course of action. However, to know the reading level of an eleventh-grade chemistry class and then to compare this to the reading level of the chemistry textbooks available makes the consideration of this factor more complex. In like manner, to use the simple, informational sort of specific instructional objectives makes the task of the teacher easy. On the other hand, to identify and to know the relationship of the aforementioned simple informational objectives to general educational objectives, the interests and characteristics of the learner, and the characteristics of contemporary society, make this factor more complex.

This discussion emphasizes a basic point: The level of teacher sophistication in decision making will be related to the understanding the teacher has of influential curricular factors. Sophisticated teacher-decision making will require a careful analysis and understanding of all the factors that can be used to build a curriculum model. Also, the teacher who has a careful understanding of the factors that build a curriculum model will probably be vitally interested in decision making in order that he can employ the knowledgeable means at his disposal to move from a problem situation to a unique action pattern.

The factors involved in any curriculum model are probably the most important items to consider at this time. The relationship of these factors, one to another, is obviously debatable and does not have as great a bearing on teacher decision making as do the factors themselves. It is not our intent to discuss theoretical factors and curricular facts as they relate to some design that could aid a teacher to make decisions. Many fine articles have been written about this subject, and it is not our purpose to write a detailed examination of the entire concept.[8]

Basic Factors Influencing Educational Objectives

Most of the authors who have written about screens of selection, curriculum design, or curriculum theory are in agreement regarding the basic factors which influence the objectives of

[8] For further discussions of this topic see: Ralph W. Tyler, *Basic Principles of Curriculum and Instruction* (Chicago: University of Chicago Press, 1950); *Toward Improved Curriculum Theory; Supplementary Educational Monograph Number 71*, ed. Virgil E. Herrick and Ralph W. Tyler (Chicago: University of Chicago Press, 1950); Edward A. Krug, *Curriculum Planning* (New York: Harper, 1957); and J. Galen Saylor and William M. Alexander, *Curriculum Planning for Modern Schools* (New York: Holt, Rinehart and Winston, Inc., 1966).

an educational program. Typically, these factors are listed under headings such as: (1) the philosophy of democracy or the philosophy of the "good life," (2) the basic needs of people, and (3) the characteristics of contemporary society. In some instances, the authors have combined the first and the third. In other instances, the concepts of major social functions or persistent life situations are related to the first and the third items listed. Some authors not only discuss the basic needs of the people but also add to this bracket their discussion of the characteristics of the learner. At this point, we have no basic quarrel with any of these concepts. Our concern is the realization that careful knowledge of the specific basic factors which influence the definition of educational objectives are considered necessary for teacher decision making.

Basic Factors Influencing the Development of a Teaching-Learning Situation

The first three factors listed above help to define the task of an educational program. However, after general educational objectives have been identified and translated into grade level and/or departmental objectives, and, after these have then been translated into specific instructional objectives for the classroom, the subobjectives are influenced by a series of other factors. Some of these are: (1) the nature of the learner, (2) theories of learning and instruction, (3) physical facilities, (4)administrative and supervisory practices, and (5) curricular approaches.

Again, our concern is not to organize these factors into a specific model but rather to point them out, generally, as areas which influence teachers in their decision-making processes. These thought-provoking factors cannot be ignored; and the contemporary teacher does not wish to ignore them as he considers the specific instructional objectives, the subject-matter content which will serve as a vehicle for the objectives, the techniques he will use as he works with students, the instructional materials he will use, and the measuring devices he will use to discover if the objectives have been achieved.

When he employs these factors to develop a better educational program, what other prior choices must he consider? As

with Dewey and his teaching staff in the experimental laboratory school in Chicago, what global questions and problems exist that need answers? What over-all choices must be contemplated in order to improve instruction in the classroom, laboratory, and study center?

QUESTIONS AND PROBLEMS THAT NEED TOTAL STAFF INVOLVEMENT

Perhaps it is wise in beginning this section to again quote John Dewey in order to re-emphasize, first, the role of his teachers in the laboratory school and, second, to identify the four basic questions or problems which served as a basis for their exploration.

It has been popularly assumed that I am the author of these ready-made ideas and principles which were to go into execution. I take this opportunity to say that the educational conduct of the school, as well as its administration, the selection of subject-matter, and the working out of the course of study, as well as actual instruction of children, have been almost entirely in the hands of the teachers of the school; and that there has been a gradual development of the educational principles and the methods involved, not a fixed equipment. The teacher started with question marks, rather than with fixed rules, and if any answers have been reached, it is the teachers of the school who have supplied them. We started on the whole with four such questions, or problems:

I. What can be done, and how can it be done, to bring the school into closer relation with the home and neighborhood life —instead of having the school a place where the child comes solely to learn certain lessons? What can be done to break down the barriers which have unfortunately come to separate the school life from the rest of the everyday life of the child? . . .

II. What can be done in the way of introducing subject-matter in history and science and art, that shall have a positive value and real significance in the child's own life; that shall represent even to the youngest children, something worthy of attainment in skill or knowledge; as much so to the little pupils as are the studies of the high school or college student to him? . . .

III. How can instruction in these formal, symbolic branches —the mastering of the ability to read, write, and use figures intelligently—be carried on with everyday experience and occupation as their background and indefinite relations to other studies of more inherent content, and be carried on in such a way that the child shall feel the necessity through their connection with subjects which appeal to him on their own account? . . .

IV. Individual attention. This is secured by small grouping—eight or ten in a class—and a large number of teachers supervising systematically the intellectual needs and attainments and critical well-being and growth of the child. . . . It requires but a few words to make this statement about attention to individual powers and needs, and yet the whole of the school's aim and methods, moral, physical, intellectual, are bound up in it.[9]

In public education today the elusive answers to these old questions are still being sought, and there are many more questions and problems that must be explored. If all of these questions and problems are not explored cooperatively by the staffs in elementary and secondary education, then teacher decision making on the classroom level of operation will suffer accordingly. Contrary to the status of professional education in Dewey's time, the study of the global questions and problems related to individual teacher decision making today would not only be studied by a staff in an experimental laboratory school, but would be studied, or should be studied, by the staff of any school. Today's level of professional staff competence and the growth of professional knowledge, as well as the development of curriculum and instructional theory, have led us to the point where we can no longer leave the identification and solution of larger instructional questions and problems to a single group of professional educators such as a national commission, a group of administrators, or the textbook writers. Finding the answers to questions and problems which will influence decision making on the classroom level of operation requires teacher involvement and participation. Stated succinctly, the teacher's professional ability must be brought to bear on such questions and problems for a very simple reason: the answers to instructional questions and problems have a

---

[9] John Dewey, *The School and Society* (New York: McClure, Phillips and Co., 1900), pp. 115–19.

direct relationship to increasing or decreasing the amount and quality of teacher decision making at the classroom level. In today's professional education world, seeking answers to questions and problems that promote further decision making on the classroom level of operation is necessary and realistic. It is inconceivable that the professional teacher in today's educational world would allow instructional decision making by groups except as decisions of groups supplement the planning needs of the teacher.

The following eight global questions pertain to pupil learning since teacher decision making on the classroom level of operation revolves about the organization of teaching-learning situations for pupils. In other words, these questions or problems are directly related to the improvement of the instructional program, but the general scope of the questions and problems is so large that they require general staff involvement because of their bearing and influence on the teaching-learning situations planned by an individual teacher.

1. *Can objectives of education for a total school program grow out of a definition of individual objectives for a learner?* Notice that the above question pertains to objectives of education for individual pupils. In the past, most thinking related to educational goals has revolved about large groups of students. Over-all decision-making in this area may facilitate the work of the individual teacher. But, a basic question must be answered: how can we ever make the transition so that the definition of the general goals for a secondary school or an elementary school grows out of the specific goals for an individual learner? At the present time, the reverse is true. School staffs have never really thought this way before. Thus far, in educational planning, attention has always been given to a description of the general objectives for a school. From this general list, grade levels and separate departments have identified their objectives. From the grade or departmental level lists, have grown the specific instructional objectives for the classroom. When a clear relationship existed, the situation was considered satisfactory. Now, however, in relation to the question posed above, perhaps the time has come to reconsider the order of development.

Perhaps such a logical or orderly growth, from general to area to classroom, stands clearly in the path of teacher decision making. Perhaps serious thought about the individual student has been lost in the gradation of objectives, themselves. Perhaps serious thinking about the individual learner, his needs, interests, and abilities should define specific instructional objectives for that learner. Commonality of individual pupils' objectives should lead to something akin to grade levels, departmental areas, or phases. From further commonality should come the over-all objectives or purposes of a specific school. Perhaps, in reality, the general goals for a school cannot be defined first. Perhaps the general goals for a school must be defined after the objectives have been specified for one individual learner, another individual learner, and another, and so on.[10] Then, it is conceivable that the broad list of goals might be quite similar to today's goals. However, the reverse emphasis in development would place major responsibility for decision making on the classroom teacher. Perhaps this should be the process for which we should strive.

People who live in our society share common experiences, common activities, and common goals; but, basically, they play separate roles as individuals. Very simply, an individual votes as an individual. It is also true that a group votes, but it is the individual in the group who makes the contribution to that vote. He has to make up his mind. This is the way it should be in a democracy where there is concern for the human dignity of an individual person. When one considers carefully the aspects of democracy, the dignity of a human being, and human dignity in terms of an educational institution, a point is reached where, philosophically, the goals or objectives should not be defined for a total school population until the definitions have grown out of a realization that many individual goals are common.

Surely this prime question needs thought and action.

---

[10] These points are implicit, if not explicit in two yearbooks: National Society for the Study of Education, *Individualizing Instruction, Sixty-first Yearbook, Part I* (Chicago: The Association, 1962); and Association for Supervision and Curriculum Development, *Individualizing Instruction* (Washington, D.C.: The Association, 1964).

Teacher decision making cannot be hung-up on a seemingly illogical approach to thinking about so important a subject as the task of the school.

In trying to answer this question, one must recognize that although the thrust is toward individualized instruction, no answer seeks the destruction of students' learning the skills of group sharing or community planning, which are necessary in order to preserve and maintain a society. Rather, a sense of direction regarding teacher decision making for the welfare of the individual is emphasized to counterbalance the present educational format centered on group objectives alone. As of this writing there are three projects that hold distinct promise for helping teachers design, identify, and choose individual objectives for each pupil in terms of the characteristics of a pupil.[11] All these projects employ the computer as a planning aid. Perhaps the use of high-speed electronic data processing to accomplish this task indicates how difficult, if not impossible, it is to answer this question without an ideal retrieval system which is capable of performing millions of man-hours of work in a single hour. In all of these research-oriented projects the primary emphasis is on helping a specific teacher, or a teacher team, preplan teaching-learning situations for individual students. The electronic data processing machinery, reacting to a tremendous memory bank of pertinent objectives, content, instructional methods, and materials, retrieves for the teacher specific teaching-learning suggestions that are related to specific instructional objectives chosen for the student by the teacher, chosen by the teacher and the student working together, or chosen by the pupil, himself. (According to one study covered in "Use of the Computer in Curriculum Planning," objectives can be selected by the computer since it is programmed to retrieve items related to the pupil's specific individual characteristics.) Without computer assistance this process seems impossible.

We are emphasizing that the answer to the question posed lies in the potential utilization of electronic data processing in

---

[11] Robert S. Harnack, "Use of the Computer in Curriculum Planning," *International Review of Education,* special issue in process on "Uses and Value of the Computer in Education."

order that the teacher has at his fingertips suggestions of specific instructional objectives related to the abilities, interests, desires, wants, and needs of a group of students. Computers are a fascinating tool. Evidence indicates that they will help to answer this question, provided that concerted efforts are made by professional educators to develop materials, ideas, and processes that are theoretically sound, truly helpful for the teacher, and within a reasonable cost factor.

2. *Can scope and sequence curricular patterns be developed which are related to the individual pupil as well as to elements such as major social functions, developmental tasks, theories of learning, and the reorganized patterns of subject matter areas? Can such patterns of scope and sequence be made applicable to the individual learner? If such patterns of scope and sequence are made applicable to the individual learner, can they also be made applicable to the small group and the large group?* If an answer can be found to the first question posed—yes, we can define objectives for each individual, and from this herculean task will grow general objectives. If we answer that way, then in like manner fruitful exploration can begin regarding the scope and sequence. Basically, a scope and sequence for an individual pupil would be related directly to his objectives with careful consideration given to the other factors mentioned.

We may discover that present scope and sequence plans are useless when true individualization of instruction is the rule. We may discover that scope and sequence plans which delineate a series of teaching-learning situations for a period of time and in a particular order, and which may be justified by a subject matter area organization, the expanding world of a group of learners, or the persistent life situations of people living in a democracy, are difficult to apply to individual learners. Individual teaching-learning plans which bear on present organizational concepts may be consistently unrealistic and unimaginative because they are conceived within a narrow framework of the general scope and sequence organized for large groups of learners. We may discover that any crystallized scope and sequence used as a basis for defining a series of teaching-learning situations for a learner is outmoded and unnecessary. Therefore, the time may come when professional staffs no longer seek or need a definition of scope and sequence for a large group of pupils. What a confusing school we might have! But, how very real it might be!

If we agree that "good" education means the education of an individual in terms of his interests, needs, wants, and desires, school staffs will have to take the next step: not merely think about individual differences or the range of student differences, but act according to the differences. Thought will be focused on educating the individual and planning the actual definition of *his* objectives, the definition of *his* scope and sequence, the definition of *his* subject matter, the definition of *his* activities, and the like. Some schools are trying to do this.[12] Different scopes and sequences, or various phases, exist for the learner in a few situations. Other schools allow the student to change his daily schedule after short notice. A planned change in a daily schedule combined with a different concept of staff utilization, plus large group, small group, and independent study combined with the various phases of scope and sequence, indicates that answers can be found. Perhaps the definition of the scope and sequence for an individual pupil is "around the corner."

If the answer to our second question is discovered, it will be related to the emerging needs curricular approach, an intelligent and imaginative teaching staff, and excellent supportive services that range from computer assistance to time for pre-planning. Any hardheaded realist in curriculum planning knows these factors are a long way from reality. Nevertheless, he would readily emphasize that any determination of scope and sequence, or curricular organization, would have to be built around the needs, interests, concerns, and problems of students involved in meeting day-to-day situations in society. The scope of the curriculum would be the scope of the student's experience at any given time. He would agree that the scope of the curricular organization or pattern would broaden and deepen rapidly as experiences with society expand. Obviously, the frame of reference on which he would build this organizational pattern would be the identification of specific

---

[12] For a comprehensive review of these activities in various schools see: Gail Inlow, *The Emergent in Curriculum* (New York: John Wiley and Sons, Inc., 1966).

instructional individual objectives designed to help students identify and define their needs, problems, and interests.

Looking for an answer does not mean we "start from scratch." It means that we first rediscover those concepts which have been written about many times but have never been truly a part of the American educational scene. For example: the child-centered school, the community-centered school, the pattern of the eight-year study, and the core programs. No one can truthfully say that we have "passed through" these periods in American education. In reality, there has been much wheel-spinning and much writing, but very little follow-up on sporadic attempts to define scope and sequence for an individual pupil—attempts which some day may gain prominence through historical perspective.

In order to answer questions one and two in any significant way, we must have knowledge of the emerging needs approach, documented information about pupils, the process of pupil-teacher planning, and a flexibility of work and spirit. What is so frustrating is the fact that the answers to these first two questions had been partially found in the past only to be buried in a rubble generated by very real logistic problems which, in professional education today, we can overcome.

3. *What kinds of information about the characteristics of individual pupils must be gathered by a school system in order to facilitate teacher decision-making on the classroom level?* At the present time school systems have amassed great quantities of information about pupils. However, in most instances, the information is useless to teachers planning teaching-learning situations for individual pupils or for small groups of pupils. In practice, the best indicator for teacher decision making seems to be the immediate interest level and reading level of the student.

The considered efforts of research staffs must study these variables, or factors, related to the characteristics of the learner in order to help the teacher find ways to use this information in regard to decision making for the improvement of teaching-learning situations. At the present time, most teachers can see a relationship between basic intelligence and the content of subject matter. Basic intelligence seems to indicate whether or not a specific learner can absorb certain abstract content. The farther down the intelligence scale one goes, according to most teachers, the less ability the specific student has for absorbing subject matter that is not concrete. In other words, teacher decision making related to subject-matter content, *per se,* would cause a teacher to shy away from using abstract concepts with lower I.Q. students. He would move from the abstract concepts, to the relative concepts, to the concrete facts as he moved down the I.Q. scale.

What must be explored are the other areas which may help to describe for teachers those characteristics of students helpful in defining the teaching-learning situation. Social class background is a case in point. When a teacher is involved in making a decision, what should it mean to him to have a child who comes from a higher class background? What should it mean to a teacher who is making a decision about a book he may use? Given a certain social class background, what objectives from a unit might be chosen? Similar questions must be asked about terms such as aggressive behavior, withdrawn behavior, and the like. The basic point in all this is fascinating. We have studied, written, and debated the concept of individual differences for years. Yet, when we consider teacher decision making at the "point of impact"—which is the actual planning for the classroom—we are often hard-pressed to say what these characteristics will mean for choosing objectives, content, developmental activities, instructional materials, and all of the unmentioned aspects which constitute the teaching-learning situation.

Perhaps the only way to overcome this dilemma is to have teachers work out the answers to these questions in the classroom. Maybe teachers will indicate, as a result of being forced to make decisions, the pupil variables, factors, or characteristics about which they require knowledge. In other words, being forced to make decisions may also force the teacher to consider those pupil characteristics that, in reality, do influence the development of teaching-learning situations. And as a result of practicing decision making, teachers may indicate that they can or cannot plan certain experiences for pupils because they do or do not have necessary information about learners.

This was the tack taken by the staff of the Center for Curriculum Planning, School of Education, State University of New York at Buffalo, when they sought, with the assistance of a grant from the United States Office of Education (Cooperative Research Program, No. D-112), to demonstrate the effectiveness of applying electronic processing equipment, within the context of the unit approach, to relate preplanning of subject matter, materials, and means of presentation to the needs and receptive abilities of individual pupils and of small and large groups.[13] The emphasis of this pilot demonstration dealt specifically with a concept of individualization of instruction through unit teaching utilizing specific suggestions retrieved from computer-based resource units. (This approach is not to be confused with "computer-assisted instruction.") In order for the computer to have something to retrieve, very large resource units were developed about a specific topic, and each item in these resource units was coded in terms of three areas: the specific instructional objectives of the resource unit, itself; professional decisions that certain teachers would make; and characteristics that would describe an individual learner. Very careful thought was required to develop sets of variables related to the learner's characteristics and the type of professional decisions that teachers have to make.

At the time of original development, as a useful or potential basis for processing data, serious attention was given to the area of the individual learner's characteristics. Should it serve as a basis for processing or coding a resource unit? The staff was advised by many people that specific areas within this category were much too hazy to aid the teacher in retrieving suggestions from the resource unit. Areas such as interests, social class, intelligence, developmental tasks, handicapped behavior, and the like do not really indicate a specific course of action for the development of a teaching-learning situation. It was suggested that specific instructional objectives and professional-decision categories, only, should be used as a basis for

---

[13] Robert S. Harnack, *The Use of Electronic Computers to Improve Individualization of Instruction Through Unit Teaching* (Buffalo, N.Y.: State University of New York at Buffalo and Research Foundation of State University of New York, Cooperative Research Project No. D-112, 1965).

processing data. The staff finally decided to include the learner's characteristics as a potential basis for processing data, because such a base, although not always clearly designating specifics for a teaching-learning situation, could serve as a springboard into educational research related to a study of the learner's characteristics as they relate to the components of a teaching-learning situation. In order to include these characteristics, the following variables were identified to provide a categorical list for coding the base data necessary for the electronic memory banks.

I.Q.
00 (75–89)
01 (90–109)
02 (110–130)
03 (above 130)

Social Class
05 (Lower–lower)
06 (Upper–lower)
07 (Lower–middle)
08 (Upper–middle)
09 (Lower–upper)
10 (Upper–upper)

Reading Level
(Secondary School)
12 (Below 7th grade)
13 (7th grade)
14 (8th grade)
15 (9th grade)
16 (10th grade)
17 (11th grade)
18 (12th grade)
19 (Above 12th grade)

Reading Level
(Elementary School)
20 (1st grade)
21 (2nd grade)
22 (3rd grade)
23 (4th grade)
24 (5th grade)
25 (6th grade)
26 (Above 6th grade)

Sex
27 (Male)
28 (Female)

34 (11th)
35 (12th)

Grade Level
(Elementary School)
37 (1st)
38 (2nd)
39 (3rd)
40 (4th)
41 (5th)
42 (6th)

Interests (Secondary School)
130 Social Sciences
131 Physical Science
132 Natural Science
133 Humanities
134 Fiction
135 Biography
136 Autobiography
137 Poetry
138 Music
139 Math
141 Art
142 Creative Writing
143 Adventure
144 Nonfiction

Interests (Elementary School)
146 Everyday experiences
147 Early days
148 Modern wonders
149 Other places
150 Animals
151 Famous people
152 Old tales
153 Natural phenomenon
154 Fun and Humor

Grade Level (Secondary School)
  30 (7th)
  31 (8th)
  32 (9th)
  33 (10th)

155 Numbers
156 Music and Rhythm
157 Making things
158 Adventure
159 Nonfiction

Developmental Tasks (Secondary School)
  44 Accepting one's physique and achieving a masculine or feminine social role
  45 Achieving new and more mature relations with age-mates of both sexes
  46 Achieving emotional independence of parents and other adults
  47 Achieving assurance of economic independence
  48 Selecting and preparing for an occupation
  49 Developing intellectual skills and concepts necessary for civic competence
  50 Desiring and achieving socially responsible behavior
  51 Preparing for marriage and family life
  52 Acquiring a set of values and an ethical system as a guide to behavior

Developmental Tasks (Elementary School)
  54 Learning physical skills necessary for ordinary games
  55 Building wholesome attitudes toward oneself as a growing organism
  56 Learning to get along with age-mates
  57 Learning to appropriate masculine or feminine social role
  58 Developing fundamental skills in reading, writing, and calculating
  59 Developing concepts necessary for everyday living
  60 Developing conscience, morality, and a scale of values
  61 Achieving personal independence
  62 Developing attitudes toward social groups and institutions

Vital Statistics
  161 Only child
  162 Twin
  163 Oldest child
  164 Youngest child
  165 Parents separated
  166 Father deceased
  167 Mother deceased

168 Adopted child
169 Cared for by guardian
Handicap-Behavior
  170 Physical handicap
  171 Aggressive behavior
  172 Withdrawn behavior
  173 I.Q. under 75

Occupational Interests
(Secondary School)
  175 Industrial
  176 Communication
  177 Transportation
  178 Homemaking Arts
  179 Foods and Agriculture

180 Finance
181 Business & Office (also Data Processing)
182 Sales and Marketing
183 Recreation and Travel
184 Service Areas
185 Construction

As of this writing, no report can be made of findings related to learners variables since not enough evidence has been gathered on this subject. But what is important is the fact that the teachers who have used the computer-based resource units are beginning to feed back to the Center materials which indicate that certain variables about a learner are directly related to specific suggestions in a resource unit. These teachers are indicating, as a result of practicing decision making, that they can (or cannot) find certain experiences for pupils because they do (or do not) have necessary information about learners. This has caused the Center staff to modify the list of variables from time to time. The most recent modification was the addition of the list of occupational interests.

4. *Can staff utilization and the organization of the school day be improved in order to facilitate teacher decision making for individuals, small groups, and large group instruction?* The pioneering work that has already been done in this area[14] is basically sound for purposes of teacher decision making. Efforts in this area have tried to take the handcuffs off the stodgy concepts of staff utilization and school day organization in order to promote better learning for pupils. Actually, in regard to the thesis of this book, this same pioneering work has, in reality, taken the handcuffs off the teacher in terms of teacher decision making. What has been discovered has been helpful: within the construct of the large school and its "efficient" operation, it is possible to use personnel to organize the school day in such a way that individualization of instruction can become a reality.

School staffs in Ridgewood High School, Norridge, Illinois, and Melbourne High School, Melbourne, Florida, to name but two schools, must be given enormous credit for reducing the

---

[14] John I. Goodlad and Robert H. Anderson, *The Nongraded Elementary School* (New York: Harcourt, Brace and World, Inc., 1963). (Although we tend to cite the latest references, the pioneering work done by Florence Kelly of the Milwaukee Public Schools in the area of non-graded primary school cannot be ignored.) B. Frank Brown, *The Nongraded High School* (Englewood Cliffs, N.J.: Prentice-Hall, Inc., 1963); J. Lloyd Trump and Dorsey Baynham, *Focus on Change— Guide to Better Schools* (Chicago: Rand McNally and Co., 1961); and Lloyd Trump and Lois S. Karasik, *Focus on the Individual—a Leadership Responsibility* (Washington, D.C.: The National Association of Secondary School Principals, 1965).

straightjacket, hidebound, handcuff effect on teacher decision making. They have broken the crystalization of staff utilization and school organization; and, in so doing, they have made time available for teachers to practice teacher decision making. While the conventional school has approximately 7 to 11 per cent of the teachers' weekly professional time set aside for planning, Ridgewood High School has increased this percentage to approximately 35 per cent. This point cannot be ignored.

Whatever the answers may be to the questions we have posed, the purpose of all concerned must be to try to shunt any staff utilization and school organization obstacle which gets in the way of professional action by the school staff. If an administrative procedure, such as organizing a school day, gets in the way of intelligent decision making for the welfare of individual pupils, something is wrong with that administrative procedure. Basically, that procedure or organization is unsound; functionally, it is not workable; and philosophically, it runs contrary to the concept of individualization.

Again, to restate the main point, the format of the optimal school-day organization and staff utilization will probably be derived as total education staffs explore, systematically, the creative possibilities for working with students.

5. What types of instructional materials must be purchased, developed, or borrowed to facilitate teacher decision making related to the identification of educational objectives for individual pupils? In like manner, what instructional materials are necessary in terms of new information about pupils, different staff utilization, or different school organization? Think what a library would be like if it were geared to individualization of instruction! Practically every item that now exists in the library would still exist because everything now in a library is for an individual. The individual draws out books; he draws out magazines; he looks at the vertical file; he looks at reference books. But what he looks for, or at, is reading matter; it is printed material. Consider the other instructional materials used in a school situation. There are: overhead projectors, filmstrips, films, television, tapes, audio tapes, and so forth. The nonprinted instructional materials available today are for a large group of students—the total classroom. They are not made for an individual to study.

The library of the future will encourage the individual pupil to withdraw materials that can be used on an overhead projector, or a 2 by 2 inch slide, for viewing in an individual study carrel. He will withdraw a film to be viewed, individually. He will use an individual study carrel to view a television video-tape. He will take a filmstrip and view it as an individual. These procedures will take place in the library or in a study center. At the present time we have a dichotomy. The library serves printed matter to students who wish to study as individuals; an audio-visual center serves teachers instructional materials for classroom use—materials which are not available to individual pupils for study purposes. The individual student cannot check out a filmstrip, a film, a video-tape, tape recording, etc. However, because most programmed instruction is printed matter, it is available for individual consumption. An individual may go to the library to study a programmed text in Algebra III. In foreign languages, individuals can benefit from using audio laboratories although such laboratories are often used in a group situation only.

But the basic question goes beyond this. What new types of instructional materials will be made available to the individual student? Will concern be transferred to the development of films, video-tapes, programmed instruction, filmstrips, and tapes for individual pupil consumption? True concern for individualization of instruction, or true concern for professional teacher-decision making, means that the professional staff must explore the development and use of instructional materials with the individual pupil as the point of departure. All this with the recognition that the group will not be ignored if individuality is stressed. But, at the present time, the reverse is true: the individual can be, and often is, ignored if the group is stressed. In the area of instructional materials, textbooks and films for the total class have been developed. Video-tapes and filmstrips for the total class have been emphasized. What is needed, however, is diametrically opposed to current practice. The impact point must be the individual student and the instructional materials that are prepared for him—related to his individual abilities, interests, aptitudes, and needs as he grows in our society. The instructional materials must sparkle for his unique characteristics.

Perhaps the demands of teachers involved in teacher decision making will help to identify the types of instructional materials which must be constructed. For as teachers make decisions for the benefit of individual pupils, they may discover that the materials do not relate to the specific characteristics of the individual learner.

Perhaps it is unnecessary to point out that there are schools where the professional staff has thought this way. Where thinking about individual students has lead to action, teachers have pointed emphatically to the need for open individual study carrels which can transmit electronically, on call from a central control, live television programs, taped television programs, audio-taped lectures or discussions, combination audio-tapes and 2 x 2 slides via the television link, filmstrips and all types of films (16 mm, 8 mm, sound, silent, continuous loop) via the television link, and chart or overhead transparency materials. Teachers have requested and used programmed instructional materials. They have generated the development of the all-purpose general education rooms and study centers in elementary education and in all of the subject matter areas found in a secondary school. Such general education areas and study centers are stocked with working materials and apparatus for the individual student. Any visit to one of numerous schools where staffs have incorporated these ideas will help to transmit the specific descriptions of their projects which are difficult to translate into cold print.

Logistically this question can be answered. Strategically, the answer will depend on curriculum planning that emphasizes intelligent utilization of individualized instructional materials. This aspect will continue to be difficult and will probably follow a recognition by staffs of the need to first make specific instructional objective and curriculum pattern decisions for individual pupils.

The key to the successful definition of materials for individual students probably lies in the singleness of staff purpose to provide instruction for the individual student. This is a choice that an individual teacher and a total staff make. Making the choice to do something about individual teaching-learning situations is no more difficult than making a choice not to do anything about individual teaching-learning situations. However, once the choice is made to provide a learning environment for an individual student, implementation may cause a series of fascinating curriculum problems which can be treated quite intelligently without losing sight of the basic goal, the education of an individual.

Since one cannot separate (except for academic treatment) the segments of a teaching-learning situation, *methodology* as a separate entity must be thoughtfully considered along with materials of instruction, subject-matter content, and specific goals. In these pages, very few references are actually made to "how" the teacher works with an individual student or "how" the teacher works with a group of students for purposes of individualizing instruction. Generalized statements about methodology are somewhat meaningless when one tries to apply them to a specific subject-matter area or grade level. In like manner, general statements about methodology might be useless when one tries to apply them to individualization of instruction. Perhaps one generalization may be allowed: Some teachers are so delicately tuned to an individual student's interests and abilities that they could conceivably accomplish some specific instructional objectives for an individual student while he is part of a large group. On the other hand, most teachers would find it easier to satisfy specific instructional objectives for an individual student by utilizing those methodologies related to small group and independent study work. In any case, just as instructional materials must be identified for the individual student, so must the methodologies which will match the instructional materials; and the emphasis, for purposes of choosing the alternate methodologies, must still be placed on the concern for the individual student.

6. *What system-wide decisions can be made to encourage patterns of teaching-learning situations which emphasize the emerging needs curricular approach, unit teaching, and pupil-teacher planning?* The three selected methods of planning and organizing teaching-learning situations were chosen for this question because teacher decision making in these areas embodies the most concern for individualization of instruction. Also, system-wide decisions, which often do not involve teachers, have, in these areas, most

often blocked the way of progress. Most teachers can use some aspects of the needs approach, some aspect of unit teaching, and some aspect of pupil-teacher planning in any teaching-learning situation. But the Nth degree of teacher decision making to develop these activities requires careful planning beyond the level of classroom operation.

Exploration of a school curriculum may indicate that the individual teacher may not practice pupil-teacher planning, unit teaching, or the emerging needs curricular approach because prior decisions made on the system-wide level have gotten in the way. For example, a decision that a teacher must follow a specific narrow curriculum guide, syllabus, or course of study, automatically eliminates the curricular needs approach. A decision, for example, to practice unit teaching can be thwarted because of a system-wide decision to make the high school teacher teach five or six periods a day, with only one planning period in his schedule. Then, the necessary pre-planning time to do unit teaching is unavailable. The lack of instructional materials, the result of a decision made by a superintendent or a board who have decided that they could not afford to buy instructional materials, forces the teacher to conclude that he cannot practice pupil-teacher planning (in the area of materials) because such planning requires a collection of various instructional materials which can be used to study the subject matter in relation to the objectives defined.

The decision of a community not to buy, the decision by an administrator or a board to give the high school teacher a staggering teaching load, the decision to use the carnegie unit, the decision to use a city-wide course of study or syllabus, and the decision to add a vocational school or an academic school as opposed to a comprehensive high school are indicative of literally hundreds of decisions which may prevent the emerging needs curricular approach, unit teaching, or pupil-teacher planning.

The basic question is: what system-wide decisions have to be reconsidered in order for the teacher to practice these techniques? If we can find those decisions which stand in the way, perhaps new action patterns can be found which will allow a teacher to use the means he would like to use to achieve the ideal he has in mind.

No writer has the knowledge to identify those prior decisions on a system-wide level which have stunted the initiative of teachers to make classroom decisions which may improve instruction. The obvious need is for a local analysis to identify such conditions. It is not difficult to form a professional task force to find answers to these questions. Such a group can survey the teachers in a school system. When this is done, if there are negative situations to be found, they will be identified. Any of the negative features listed above could be present (and have been present) in school systems.

Speaking positively in order to answer our question, the spectrum of alternatives is pleasant to contemplate. School staff decisions could be made which emphasize, for example, system-wide curriculum planning. This decision creates a system-wide committee whose main concern is the improvement of communication and coordination between all schools, grade levels, and subject-matter areas. A positive system-wide decision could be made to help the total staff gain a firmer sense of the basic task of the schools. It is conceivable that a "hardening of the categories" condition has gradually developed which makes the over-all purposes of the school system somewhat archaic when related to the conditions of contemporary society. Still another positive decision which could be made by a system-wide group would be to develop resource units and other curriculum guides in order to provide general guideposts to teachers who need help when planning better teaching-learning situations.

One insidious decision made by some school administrators hurts professionalism the most: the decision to consider the staff as non-decision makers, i.e., a decision not to allow staff involvement in curriculum planning. Instead, the administrator makes a decision that his staff needs in-service education. "The individual teacher must grow professionally, and I must provide for this intellectual growth." But to what end? Can we assume that the end is the professional growth of the individual teacher? But, again, to what end? Can we then assume that the end is professional decision making about the education of pupils? Somehow, that end is never reached! Perhaps administrators lack the initiative to allow teachers to make decisions. The result may be that after many years of being caught in this milieu, this atmosphere, this way of operating, a tradition has evolved which leads many people to the conclusion that teachers are not capable of making good decisions. But, in reality, the atmosphere has changed, and the change is quite startling.

7. *Can measuring devices be developed which are related to the educational objectives identified for an individual student?* Generally speaking, the considerations which must be given to this area are enormous. The thoughts and actions to improve this area must be carefully planned since this question identifies areas probably as important as those involved in question number one. Certainly, the two questions are related.

This question and the next are tied closely to the general concept of evaluation.[15] The value of a specific instructional objective for an individual student must be considered, statements of behavioral criteria related to the objectives must be developed, and the measuring devices related to the behavioral criteria need to be created. The task is enormous, but this scientific endeavor needs doing before teacher decision making can become a reality.

Similar to instructional materials, the bulk of measuring devices available to the teacher are (1) related to large groups of students, and (2) related to simple skills and subject-matter outlines. If a specific student wishes to explore an interest area which is tangential to a general unit topic, the teacher is hard-pressed to find the measuring devices which will indicate the extent of progress made by this student. An analysis of any resource unit will show immediately the dearth of measuring devices about any topic for an individual pupil. Basically, when one considers teacher decision making, the unscientific process of measuring an individual pupil's growth is almost frightening. The unscientific nature of this area must be explored and analyzed by teaching staffs in order that the barriers to teacher decision making can be cut down. Consider for

---

[15] For an excellent overview of this area, see Stephen Abrahamson's chapters 12–17 in *Teaching and Learning in Medical School,* ed. George E. Miller (Cambridge, Mass.: The Harvard Press, 1961). Also, see E. R. Smith and Ralph W. Tyler, *Appraising and Recording Student Progress* (New York: Harper, 1942).

a moment the measuring devices used by a physician to examine a student's physical health. If the measuring devices were poor, a physician listening to the student's heart with a stethoscope would hear only blurred sounds; the sphygmomanometer would not register a distinct blood pressure; the electro-cardiogram would print a smooth, wavy line. In other words, the physician, unable to read his inaccurate measuring devices, would never know the scope of the individual's health.

Perhaps, in time, the practice of teacher decision making may, in and of itself, promote the development of scientific measuring devices related to specific instructional objectives for an individual student.

It is ever so disheartening to write that there is no positive answer to our seventh question. It is painful to indicate, even to oneself, that in this professional area we are inadequate. Nevertheless, the hopeful element is that the creation of measuring devices has always followed a careful analysis of goals—ends in view. To reiterate a basic scheme, perhaps to the point of boredom, the creation of measuring devices for individual students will have to follow the definition of goals for these same individuals.

8. *Can a system of reporting pupil progress to other staff members, parents, and pupils be devised which promotes teacher decision making?* The present system of reporting pupil progress, especially the arbitrary present system of grading, runs contrary to the whole concept of teacher decision making or the right or responsibility of an individual teacher to make an individual teaching-learning decision for an individual pupil and to follow through. The grading process itself forces a teacher who wishes to make fine gradations in terms of objectives, content, activities, materials, and measuring devices to dump everything together into something similar to a can of worms. This procedure is completely detrimental to decision making. Grading, in and of itself, is arbitrary. Certainly, such arbitrariness is detrimental enough, but this is not the basic rub. The entire concept of reporting pupil progress runs contrary to careful choosing and selecting because the teacher is forced to make a single symbol represent a thousand conditions for each individual student. Consider the complex process called learning;

consider the complex human being (the pupil) with his varied characteristics; consider a highly complex environmental item called the teaching-learning situation, which is related to the general task of the school. Now, multiply these considerations by the number of teaching-learning situations in one day, and further multiply this by the number of days in the semester. Out of all this the conscientious teacher must strive to identify a single symbol called a grade. This grade then represents the growth of a specific learner in relation to a set of goals developed by way of a very complex set of factors. Insidiously, this procedure destroys the teacher's belief in making choices and decisions for individual learners. This procedure runs counter to the very concept of individualizing instruction.

The teacher does not want his report of pupil progress to represent a "can of worms" any more than a physician would think of giving a letter grade after a three-day medical examination. If, after the examination, the physician said, "C plus," his fee might never be paid. In like manner, teachers want the means to make a comprehensive report of pupil progress for the benefit of other staff members, parents, and pupils. Actually, we have moved in this direction in many areas of education. The parent conferences on the primary school level, especially, have moved in this direction. Some employers and university officials have asked for more complete reports of progress. These are steps in the proper direction, but they are small steps.

The answers to our eighth question probably will be found by professional staff members who show a concern for an individual pupil's growth. Then, discussion will center about the growth of one learner from level A to level B. Such thinking might break the spell. Level A will represent the pupil's knowledge before the teaching-learning situations were used, and level B will represent his growth in terms of the teaching-learning situations. The discussion will not center about the growth of the learner in relation to a group norm. Again, we can reasonably assume that this type of thinking will follow individual choices made in regard to objectives, content, activities, materials, and measuring devices. After such preliminary decision making by a staff member, he might think it ridiculous to use a general, arbitrary, single symbol to represent a highly complex set of functions.

SUMMARY

The *concept* of involving teachers in curriculum is old, but the *practice* of involving teachers in the improvement of instruction is still new and sporadic. Where teachers have tried to improve instruction and have had a free reign to make choices for the benefit of students, some prior decisions made by teachers, administrators, boards of education, and the supportive services may have blocked the way for improving or fostering teacher decision making. Such prior decisions must be identified and questioned.

Basically, these decisions must be identified, questioned, studied, and changed because their existence has caused professional teachers who wish to improve instruction to become cynical about their role as scientific workers. These teachers must have the opportunity to question the validity of prior decisions. Teachers who have been involved in curriculum planning have tried to do this and in many instances have been successful. Obviously, the hope is that all teachers will accept the challenge.

Perhaps all teachers will not fit this mold, but certainly those who do can be called professional. In any profession there are laggards, indifferent workers, and irresponsible misfits. Here, we are discussing the role of teachers who are experienced and who have assumed the responsibility for the improvement of instruction. These are the people who must pose questions similar to the eight asked in this chapter, and these are the people who must then get at the task of curriculum planning.

CHAPTER THREE

THE TEACHER AND THE CURRICULUM-PLANNING PROCESS

Probably the first thing to do in establishing a clear understanding of the planning process in local government is to brush aside a lot of the hokum that still clings to the idea of planning: the hokum associated with static master plans manufactured by peripatetic high priests of planning; the hokum that planning is a mysterious science and art that can be practiced only by those who have undergone some sort of special intellectual circumcision for the purpose; the hokum that planning has some ethereal quality that cannot stand being subjected to the rugged processes of democratic government.

. . . And it is no worse than the delusions that are its converse: the delusion that planning, being common sense, is only that and requires no special knowledge: the delusion that the longing of a child for a place in which to play has less validity than a decision by the community that it cannot afford to provide it.[1]

Curriculum planning, similar to community planning, needs to be thought of as a guiding philosophy for educators. Curriculum planning is the frame of reference in which professional staff members work. It is their format for professional operations. The "hokum" and "delusions," referred to above by authors discussing urban planning, apply to school planning as well. The purpose of this chapter, therefore, is twofold.

---

[1] *An Approach to Urban Planning,* ed. Gerald Breese and Dorothy E. Whiteman (Princeton, N.J.: Princeton University Press, 1953).

44

First, to emphasize the planning process as a way for professionals to work in the public school setting, and second, to understand the precise facets of the planning process in public education in order to eliminate the miserable confusion.

Myriad items describing local school curriculum changes exist in periodicals, professional books, yearbooks, and local news publications. Often these changes result from a clear faith in and an understanding of the curriculum planning process. In other instances these changes stem from administrative edict, minority group pressures on boards of education, state education department pronouncements to local schools, national committee decisions, textbook writers, or the decisions of individual teachers—decisions based on in-service education, professional reading, or graduate study. In public education, uncoordinated decision-making by numerous persons is common. Our obvious concern revolves about the many instances where decisions are made without a belief in and a knowledge of the planning process itself. When this unsatisfactory condition persists, we jeopardize both accomplishing the task of the school and cooperatively utilizing the potential of the educational teaching staff with their specialized knowledge and experience in diverse fields. Beyond this, there is a possible concomitant loss to the total educational process: the loss of a utilization of democratic planning with pupils in the classroom—a behavior first learned by the teachers as they, themselves, work together.

Accomplishing the task of the school demands a process whereby staff members can systematically evolve the plan of attack. Obviously, no one member of a teaching staff can achieve the goals of the school program. In like manner, it is highly improbable that a systematic master plan can be implemented when the individuals responsible for classroom implementation are professional workers who readily recognize the limitations of educational plans conceived without their involvement. Because, in public education, a set of general goals exist, the attainment of those goals requires some cooperative planning process involving those workers who have the responsibility to implement the attainment of the goals. Or, looking at the other side of the coin, the general goals of public education will never be reached if some means is not found to involve the workers responsible for the attainment of the goals.

Once systematic curriculum planning is understood and practiced, once the task of the school is cooperatively parcelled into its component parts, then smaller groups of teachers can plan for their specific areas, and the individual teacher can make immediate plans and decisions for the job in the classroom. For example, when the goal of good citizenship is translated into area goals for social studies, third grade science, music, and the like, the teacher can translate the area or grade level goals into specific classroom experiences. (The entire process may be reversed, but the end goal of good citizenship remains constant.) The chain of goals then is related and unbroken, and each teacher has to plan as he moves toward the satisfaction of the over-all purpose of the educational program. Certainly, this vital procedure requires temendous "give and take" between staff members who have diversified specialized knowledge but who are, nevertheless, interested in achieving a common task. How else can a pupil be educated?

This procedure calls for cooperative and comprehensive planning that is system-wide in scope. It also calls for planning which is area-wide in scope. After these two types of planning have taken place, the teacher can, with confidence and direction, make decisions which influence his immediate task in the classroom; but he needs the cooperative curriculum planning frame of reference.[2]

---

[2] The following authors have devoted considerable time and attention to the curriculum planning frame of reference: Vernon E. Anderson, *Principles and Procedures of Curriculum Improvement* (New York: The Ronald Press Company, 1965); Ronald C. Doll, *Curriculum Improvement: Decision-Making and Process* (Boston: Allyn and Bacon, Inc., 1964); Edward A. Krug, *Curriculum Planning* (New York: Harper, 1957); Alice Miel, *Changing the Curriculum—A Social Process* (New York: D. Appleton-Century Company, Inc., 1946); Albert I. Oliver, *Curriculum Improvement: A Guide to Problems, Principles, and Procedures* (New York: Dodd, Mead and Company, 1965); J. Cecil Parker, T. Bentley Edwards, and William H. Stegeman, *Curriculum in America* (New York: Thomas Y. Crowell Company, 1962); J. Galen Saylor and William M. Alexander, *Curriculum Planning for Modern Schools* (New York: Holt, Rinehart and Winston, Inc., 1966); and Hilda Taba, *Curriculum Development Theory and Practice* (New York: Harcourt, Brace & World, Inc., 1962).

In the remaining sections of this chapter an attempt will be made to examine, in some detail, the curriculum-planning process. The hope is that a detailed examination of the process will help all staff members use the process more intelligently.

DEFINING CURRICULUM AND PLANNING

Although usage still causes considerable confusion regarding the definition of the term *curriculum,* professional writers agree on a common definition which takes the term out of the narrow *course of study* concept and makes it inclusive enough to embody all of the teaching-learning experiences guided and directed by the school. The ramifications of this short definition are probably best elaborated by the more complete but still short statement which appears in the *Evaluative Criteria.*

> The *curriculum* may be defined as all the experiences which pupils have while under the direction of the school; thus defined it includes both classroom and extra-classroom activities. All such activities should therefore promote the needs and welfare of the individual and of society. *Courses of study* may be defined as that part of the curriculum which is organized for classroom use. They suggest content, procedures, aids and materials for the use and guidance of teachers, pupils, and administrators. Thus considered they contain only part of the individual pupil's curriculum. The curriculum and courses of study should be chiefly concerned with the orientation, guidance, instruction, and participation of youth in those significant areas of living for which education should supplement the work of other social institutions.

> The results of the learning process should include (1) factual information or knowledge; (2) meaning and understanding; (3) abilities to do—knowledge and understanding combined with skill; (4) desirable attitudes—scientific, social, moral, and others; (5) worthy ideals, purposes, appreciations, and interests; and (6) resultant intelligent participation in general life activities.[3]

To define the term *planning* presents much more difficulty, if for no other reason than that most people seem to know what it means. Most people would agree with the simple definition of the term *plan—a procedure or a scheme to formulated ac-*

---

[3] Cooperative Study of Secondary School Standards, *Evaluative Criteria, 1940 Edition* (Washington, D.C.: American Council on Education, 1940), p. 31. See also *Evaluative Criteria, 1950 Edition,* p. 49.

tion. But, for many reasons, this definition is not enough. Many questions are left unanswered. For example, what procedures should be followed? Who formulates the action? Should the formulation be by edict or the result of democratic action? Should the action be the result of reflective thinking, experimentation, and logic, or is there room for rationalization, emotional responses, or habit patterns? Do subject-matter specialists make the plans? Should a teacher group formulate the action pattern regardless of what the experts say? The definition of the term *planning* must be tied to assumptions about public education, the professional aspects of education, the role of democracy in education, group dynamics, and the role of the scientific teacher.

Rather than attempt to define *planning* in a few short words, some time will be spent in a piecemeal examination of its component parts. To accomplish this, we will focus on a fourfold concept of *planning* which emphasizes (a) group involvement and consensus, (b) use of expert knowledge, (c) the development and execution of specific plans, and (d) appraising plans of action.

Utilizing the Democratic Process

The first component of the term *planning* revolves about a concern for the procedures inherent in the philosophy of democracy. Part and parcel of the planning concept is wrapped in the belief that action should be the result of staff members working together to meet their immediate and long-term needs. The term "working together" is certainly trite. But the basic meaning and concepts of democracy are still real and relevant—an integral part of the *planning* definition. Briefly stated, this aspect of the definition means that staff members involved in the execution of the action proposed will have a distinct responsibility to help arrive at the decisions through the concerted effort of the total group to establish some consensus about each specific plan. The execution of this concept requires (a) that each member of the planning team will have respect for other members, (b) that all members of the planning team will use human intelligence to identify the "bold and imaginative" plans that evolve (more about this later), and (c) that the procedural emphasis involved in this democratic process will focus on the principles of group action.

What this means for local schools almost goes without saying. It means that staff members who have a direct relationship to the execution of curricular plans will be involved in the developmental and decision-making stage of such plans. It also seems obvious that not all staff members can be involved directly. Since this is the case, their representatives will serve. For example, decisions to select a common textbook, or decisions relative to the scope and sequence of arithmetic, require that the representatives of the staff concerned with the teaching and supervision of these areas be involved in the planning stage, decision stage, and execution stage of the total planning process.

Utilizing Expert Knowledge

A second aspect of the definition of *planning* revolves about the intelligent use of knowledge. Knowledge can be found in many places: in printed pages, research studies, or in the minds of people called consultants or resource people. The resource people may be members of the local school staff, the community, or university personnel. In any case, what is important in this phase of the definition is a consideration of how this knowledge is used. A few years ago, and to some extent even today, a few individuals with expert knowledge about some aspect of public education could control an entire phase of a school's instructional program. A textbook writer could control the organization of subject matter for a large group of pupils. A course-of-study outline developed by a national committee or a state group could control the subject matter for a large group of teachers. In all this, expert knowledge was tapped, but not in a way which encouraged local school curriculum planning. Expert knowledge was not scrutinized carefully by the local teachers in order that they could make judgments regarding the usefulness, application, and possible adaptation of this knowledge to the local scene.

In other words, there has never been anything wrong with expert knowledge. It has always been needed; it will always be needed. The question is: How applicable is it to the local situation? The local group should answer this question. They must have the opportunity to screen expert information and knowledge in relation to the limiting and facilitating aspects of the immediate situation. How difficult it would be to estimate the number of planning sins which have been committed by the improper use of expert knowledge. Expert knowledge about subject-matter areas, child psychology, and instructional materials and methods (to name just a few areas of concern to the local school staff) has been forthcoming for many years. The local group must be aware of this knowledge, know its advantages and limitations, and decide how this knowledge can be used to improve the instructional program. Such activity is indicative of professional behavior.

Another sin is committed when a teaching staff blithely ignores expert knowledge entirely. Education staffs, similar to the working force in the other professions, have committed this sin often. Perhaps this is human nature. Perhaps it is upsetting to change traditional operating procedures. All this (adapting the "new curriculum") makes for insecurities, and no one wants the rug pulled out from underneath him. Often, the new "syllabus," which the local teacher was supposed to have followed without being involved in the decision, certainly would make for insecurity. There was a good reason to ignore the expert who wrote a new "syllabus." He "changed" subject matter. No wonder groans come from faculty members suddenly informed about the latest "curriculum" changes to "take effect immediately." The staff had no voice in the plans. There was reason to feel insecure. There was reason to develop hostile tendencies.

Nevertheless, expert knowledge is necessary and vital for the advancement of any professional worker. The utilization of it, in terms of local conditions, needs to be an integral part of the planning definition and process. To the practical man this point almost goes without saying. Certainly, a knowledge and understanding of the background of an area is necessary before any plans can be developed. Expert knowledge is brought into focus for the planners. The knowledge of the scholars, philosophers, and scientists is analyzed and organized. This knowledge is available and must be used by the planner. If he does not have it, he must know where to find it. If the knowledge does not exist, then the theoretical aspects must be thought through; and proper research activities must be developed.

In any event, knowledge must serve as background data. If it is not used, much time, energy, and money are wasted as the so-called "planners" try to "discover and organize" knowledge which was discovered and organized many times before. Many examples exist to point up this waste. Such curriculum committee activities as improving the reporting of pupil progress to parents, providing programs for gifted children, developing a science program for elementary children, or providing foreign language instruction for young children are but a few problem areas which have been defined by professional staffs as worthwhile areas which need specific plans to overcome deficiencies. Many committee members have wasted time on these vital areas because they have not had or used background data. They did not know what had been done in hundreds of other communities, or they did not have knowledge of supplementary reading lists already available—to mention but a few reasons. In all of these instances, background data could cause a rapid movement toward a set of specific plans.

Again a warning must be re-emphasized. Expert knowledge must be used intelligently by the planners. The knowledge is there, but it must be used with discretion by the local people. Background data may or may not be applicable to the local situation. This decision must be made by the planners, but they cannot make this basic decision if they do not have the background data with which to make it. A plan for individualizing instruction used in community X may have little application for community Y. A special idea for improving an academic program for children in community A may have no relevance for community B. However, a look at the other side of the coin might indicate that something in the other plans may provide a clue for the development of local plans to overcome a serious instructional problem. Failure to review other plans may mean that the local planning staff may apply themselves for many hundreds of hours in order to complete a task which is a duplication of that which has been done before.

There are practical means whereby background information can be found in a short time. First, reference books and periodicals can be checked. *The Encyclopedia of Educational Research* can be used as well as the *Readers' Guide and Educational Index*. Periodicals such as the *Review of Educational Research* can help. Yearbooks, such as those issued by the Association for Supervision and Curriculum Development and the National Society for the Study of Education, provide background data and ideas. Beyond this there are hundreds of professional periodicals, yearbooks, and pamphlets which provide information to planners. Furthermore, as was written earlier, local university staff members in any of the subject-matter areas, as well as the staff members of professional schools, can provide excellent background data for a planning meeting. The point is that background data are readily available to the planning group, but their use must be encouraged.

Within a competent instructional materials center or curriculum laboratory, teachers should have access to a complete file, from other states and communities, of curriculum bulletins related to the local situation. In these bulletins from other local communities, state education departments, county districts, and study councils, a local staff may find the riches of professional experiences that range from school curriculum guides to suggestions for teaching extracurricular or co-curricular activities.

Developing and Executing Plans

Another aspect of the *planning* definition must be the actual development and execution of plans. Many a cynical definition of a committee has been coined by individuals involved in so-called curriculum planning who have had unsatisfactory experiences regarding the actual development and execution of curricular plans. How many times have we watched committees of teachers struggle with topics which started on cloud nine and ended at the same point? No action was ever taken. The plans were never put into effect. The end result of the committee's activity was the in-service education of the members: the resultant professional growth of the individual teachers on the committee. *But this was not curriculum planning. This was in-service education.* The end goal of such activity, professional growth, is not a part of the definition of *planning.* Planning activities require that plans be suggested, developed, and executed.

We have no genuine quarrel with committee meetings that have as their purpose in-service education of the staff. However, we think that this purpose must first be acceptable to committee members. Knowing the end goal does not then justify venting the spleen with misinterpretations of the meaning of a committee and devolping what has been referred to as "committeeitus." Members who know that the end goal of a series of committee meetings will be the formulation of plans can only vent their spleens if they have not themselves succeeded. Low teacher morale is often the result of being tricked into "planning" activities where the prime goal was not clearly defined.

At times a foolish, autocratic administrative philosophy may interfere with the development and execution of plans. Some school superintendents, principals, and supervisors think mere involvement of staff members in curriculum planning activities is fashionable. Following the development of staff plans, these administrators are hesitant to accept the plans for execution. Result: the plans gather dust in the administrator's office, and the faculty group never hears of them again. Result: faculty cynicism toward curriculum planning activities. In reality, the cynicism should be aimed at the autocratic administrator's behavior.

Appraising the Need for Readjusting Plans

Once a scheme of action has been formulated, and action taken, a continuous check is required to observe what actually occurs. This fourth point emphasizes an important principle of curriculum planning which has been called *continuity.* Generally speaking, sporadic attempts at curriculum planning tend to develop a patchwork quilt type of curriculum design which is contrary to any attempts toward systematic instruction in a school organization. The lack of continuous activity does even more than make a mixed-up design in that the planners themselves feel a sense of futility since they cannot "check out" the results of their planning.

A scheme of action usually indicates a course of action which will tend to alleviate the problem or the original cause for taking action. Such plans, therefore, contain a predictive quality. This degree of prediction (or what may be expected as a result of the action about to be taken) requires careful follow-up by the planners. The original prediction may need readjustment. For example, the work of a committee of teachers, parents, or laymen concerned with reporting pupil progress to parents may result in a scheme of action (plans) which require a change in the methods of reporting. The committee may recommend a set of report card changes. Assuming that the plans were executed and the new report card printed and used, failure to appraise the need for further change in the report card might lead to serious consequences. The action originally taken may have led to consequences (problem situations) which were much worse than the original problem situation that led to the formation of the committee. Parents, for example, might find the new report card so difficult to understand that now communication between the school staff and the home has been completely blocked.

In the above example, a simple decision to continue the work of the committee in order to appraise the need for readjusting the original plans could have prevented a series of serious problems from developing.

The above points all tie together. An understanding by the educational staff to appraise the need for the readjustment of plans indicates a sincere, scientific attitude toward planning. It also indicates that the staff intends to execute plans which have been carefully developed. Such feelings generate, in turn, the staff's intentions to think seriously about the expert knowledge needed and how this knowledge might be used. Intentions to use expert knowledge intelligently seems to indicate a belief that plans should be made to overcome the problems at hand. Basically, this points to a powerful desire on the part of the professional staff to (a) carry out the task of the school and (b) seek out, cooperatively, those problem areas within the instructional program which are hindering the school staff from accomplishing this task. Now the staff has adopted a way of thinking, a philosophy, a belief, perhaps even a faith: a way of thinking which indicates that *planning* requires involvement, expert knowledge, development and execution of plans, and the continuity which helps to check the schemes of action or the predictions which the staff has made.

Now, perhaps, it is possible to define educational *planning* as staff-centered problem solving activities which develop and execute schemes of actions needing continuous appraisal.

USING THE CURRICULUM-PLANNING PROCESS

A preflight check-off list for a pilot of a jetliner indicates procedures which should be followed before take-off. In this way he can determine, systematically, the proper conditions for safe flight. In curriculum planning, suggestions made for the utilization of the planning process could be formally itemized in like manner, but they may be of little value because of the indeterminate number of human factors which might change the immediate situation and make the formal list difficult to follow.[4] The diagrams and the explanations which follow attempt to expand and make clear the discussion of the planning process described in the preceding section. The diagrams which cover the next two pages should be considered as a single diagram. The first page itemizes, in separate squares, the main facets of the planning process which have just been described. The wavy arrows emanating from the total area called the *Planning Process* are meant to show that *all* facets of the process should penetrate *all* items and steps on the following page. If, for example, the task is to identify curricular problems or to work through some aspect of scope and sequence, all factors in the planning process should be brought to bear whenever possible.

---

[4] Parker's guidelines for curriculum development activities may prove helpful to curriculum workers. See: Parker, Edwards, and Stegeman, *Curriculum in America* (New York: Thomas Y. Crowell Company, 1962), pp. 123–28.

Whenever one divorces himself from the reality of curriculum planning and draws a diagram to illustrate a scheme of action, there is a slight danger that the academic approach may be taken literally, that the items and the order of the items may be taken as always prevailing in the indicated sequence. In reality, there are times when only certain items are at work or need working on. Other items, or parts of the process, may be temporarily ignored. Individuals actually involved in curriculum improvement may skip through certain sequences with no formal thought or time given to them. This does not mean that such individuals are ignoring or disregarding the academic schema presented here. Our only hope in presenting this picture of an action pattern lies in the increased understanding which may result from not only labelling the items but also diagraming them to emphasize a visual sequence and relationship. In the paragraphs which follow we will try to explain items and relationships which may still be unclear because of the fact that the basic task of improving teaching and learning, as an end goal, may still be quite different from

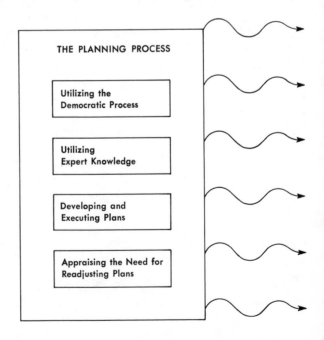

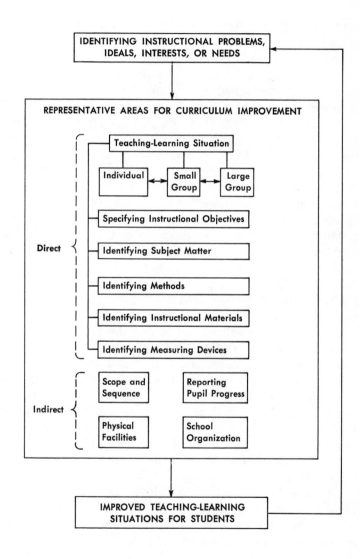

what is typically advocated in many curriculum development programs.

Identifying Instructional Problems, Ideals, Interests, or Needs

Curriculum planning is a realistic enterprise. Its main purpose is to improve the teaching-learning situations for students. The process used to accomplish this purpose is time consuming, expensive, and professionally exacting. The individuals involved want to "get down to brass tacks." As a result, the curriculum planning process grows more realistic when the individuals concerned have a distinct urge to attack instructional problems, ideals, interest areas, or needs.

The problems, interests, new ends-in-view, or need areas may evolve from consideration of a subject-matter area, its scope, sequence, relationship to the growth characteristics of children, and the like. Other problems may be concerned with instructional materials, methods, or evaluating devices. Some problems might be concerned with the definition of specific subject-area or grade-level instructional objectives. They may deal with the learning process itself. How does one teach an understanding? Or, how does one teach an appreciation? They may deal with articulation between a group of elementary schools and a junior high school, or the articulation between a high school and a college. Other problem areas might revolve around curricular experiences provided by special teachers in an elementary school or the use of consultants in the elementary school. Staff workers on the secondary school level might be concerned with an examination of independent study, modular scheduling, or team teaching. Whatever the area, the problems (interests and needs) of the professional staff become the focal point of the initial phase of the curriculum planning process.

At times, laymen define the initial stage of curriculum planning. Working with professionals, laymen define either a single new general objective of education or redefine a series of over-all tasks for the school. The definition of such general objectives related to teaching about science and the scientific attitude, consumer education, or driver education are distinct cases in point. Following the definition of broad goals, it becomes necessary for the staff to translate these objectives of education, as defined by laymen, into a series of detailed areas and specific instructional objectives in order that the staff can "get at" the over-all purposes in a systematic way. The education staff assumes the responsibility for which it was hired: to accomplish the task of the school as this task was and is defined by the puplic. The community people define or redefine, and the education staff translates into ongoing curricular experience. The education staff literally formulates schemes of action which they predict will accomplish the new task of the school.

Staff involvement for the purpose of specifying problems, interests, ends-in-view, and the like, is required and is normal procedure where there is concern for the planning process. The definition of planning stated in this chapter asks for staff involvement at all steps of the curriculum improvement program, including the specification of curricular problems or goals. Any school system that encourages staff decision making must encourage teacher involvement at the initial level of planning which, in this case, is the definition of interest areas for planning purposes.

There are school systems where teachers have never been involved in the definition of problems or of any other matters pertaining to a planning program. It is likely that these teachers have never been involved in any part of curriculum planning. If the staff is given the option of involvement in curriculum planning, the question often asked is: How shall we begin? One answer is to use a problem or interest census inquiry blank. Very simply, a decision is made to circulate to all staff members a single sheet of paper which each person is asked to return, unsigned, by a certain date. At the top of the paper, one can write the following sentence. "In order to improve the curriculum of this school system or in order to develop a curriculum planning program, would you please list, in order of importance to you, the three most pressing instructional problems which need the attention of the total school staff." The same type of sentence could be written for a single school, a grade level, or a subject-matter area department. The sentence does not have to request the identification of instructional problems, since certainly not all curriculum improvement is related to instructional problems. Ends-in-view could be written into the sentence. Or the staff could be asked to list their own instructional needs or interests. Whatever wording is used, in time an *ad hoc* committee, or any standing committee, will receive a comprehensive list of concrete problems which the staff thinks are worth studying. Now a staff has a common ground to begin curriculum planning activities. Where this technique has been used, it is fascinating to compile these inquiry blanks and discover that, although very little staff communication has taken place, approximately 75 per cent of the staff members will consistently identify similar instructional problems.

Where school systems have practiced systematic curriculum planning activities for a period of time, the problem census blank is usually not needed. Where groups of teachers have customarily met to discuss the various levels of decision making, communication is usually advanced enough so that instructional problems are readily identified through normal discussion at regular scheduled meetings of the groups.

Our main adverse criticism of many school systems is that the administrative staff have kept instructional problem identification as their responsibility and have not shown an eagerness to share it with the teaching staff. Perhaps this action results from the foolish notion that the discovery of problem situations indicates inefficient administration. Whatever the reason, curriculum improvement thrives on the identification of problems by the teaching staff; and, typically, they will identify a series of problems which are more related to the instructional program than would be problems administrators would identify. But, in any case, identification of these areas must be the concern of the total staff—teachers, administrators, guidance counselors, librarians, etc.

Whether the initial stage of curriculum planning derives its focus from instructional problems felt by the staff or from a definition of the over-all purposes by the layman, this initial focus is realistic and purposeful. The resultant planning activities should have, at least, this basic focus or purposefulness in order to encourage a high morale and a spirit of cooperation among staff members. When the curriculum planning goal is clear and real, the task is truly professional.

Logically, objectives of education require definition before planning can de done. Therefore, many school administrators have begun a curriculum-planning program by asking teachers to define the objectives of the school, study the objectives of the school, or write a philosophical statement about the task of the school. Contrary to popular practice, as an initial curriculum-planning activity this has no appeal to the staff. The false assumptions made by the administrator are threefold: (a) the staff does not have knowledge of the objectives of education, (b) the staff, not laymen, should define objectives of education, and (c) such an analysis will *then* enable the staff to define the teaching-learning experiences necessary to accomplish the goals. All three assumptions are subject to searching questions. In the first place, it is questionable (almost demoralizing) to think that teachers do not have some knowledge of the goals of an instructional program. Furthermore, a redefinition of goals at an early stage of planning—a stage that has not defined the instructional problems—would merely cause a restatement of original impressions.

Certainly, the over-all objectives of an educational program are important, but they are not important *per se*. They derive their importance as they help a professional staff define a course of action. When a scheme of action is about to be formulated, when predictions to overcome an instructional problem are made, an objective of education serves as a criterion to help the staff make a value judgment regarding the effectiveness of the suggestions made. The objective serves as a yardstick to make judgments regarding the worthwhileness of the plan of action. Therefore, the objectives serve as tools for decision making, and when their service is needed, they must be called to action. As a result, the logic that objectives should come first is unsound because, in reality, the objectives have already come first as a result of hundreds of years of ongoing instructional activities in schools. (Again, however, it should be pointed out that the formulation of a new objective of education would require intensive study by the staff in order that they might translate that objective into an instructional program. However, the inclusion of new objectives of education are certainly not a common occurrence.)

Does this mean that objectives of education are never discussed? When a specific objective of education serves as a tool to help planners make decisions, this objective, *per se,* may be the focal point of a long, analytical discussion. During such a discussion the staff carefully thinks through the objectives of education, but their purpose is not to formulate a set of objectives. Instead their purpose is to analyze the meaning of the objective, to translate it into area and specific classroom objectives, to find sparkling facets in a dry, bald statement, and to judge its intent in terms of the development of information to be learned, understandings to be gained, and appreciation to be encouraged. Under these conditions the study of objectives becomes important.

Representative Areas for Curriculum Improvement

The four planning-process factors listed on the left-hand page of the original diagram impregnate every area diagrammed on the right-hand page. When one looks at the items listed under "Representative Areas for Curriculum Improvement," it is possible to recognize the general magnitude of the planning task. One sees that a cluster of planning factors have to infiltrate a large number of diverse elements which we have arbitrarily classified as areas which need improving. Also, when one looks at these curricular areas, one easily recognizes that some which probably need improvement have been left out. A specific list would be endless. After a period of time, such a list would encompass everything which makes up an all-school program in any school. Nevertheless, our purpose in the next few paragraphs is to review the influence of the planning process on a few common specific areas which constantly demand improvement.

1. *Improving teaching-learning situations for individuals, small and large groups. (These items are directly related to instruction)* Within this area, a teaching staff makes thousands of decisions daily. Certainly, in this area the planning process should be em-

ployed. Concerned with teaching-learning situations, this area not only encompasses the planning that is done for individual students, small groups, and large groups in terms of a single teaching-learning situation, but it also encompasses the planning done for many teaching-learning situations which might constitute a complete unit of work. The planning needed is directly related to the work the teacher does in the classroom and influences the decisions he makes as he works with students throughout the day. This area encompasses the planning of specific instructional objectives, subject matter to be taught, the instructional materials to be employed, the methodologies to be used, and the measuring devices, which, hopefully, will indicate the extent of learning in relation to the goals chosen. It really includes a tremendous mass of potential planning activities which require detailed attention and which need to be guided by the planning-process factors. It would seem that if these factors are not appropriately employed in this area, an area which has direct relationship to the role of the teacher as he works with boys and girls, then these same factors would have little value for the indirect areas for curriculum improvement which follow in the diagram. In like manner, it follows that if teacher involvement is not encouraged and practiced at all operational planning levels which influence this direct area, then there is little purpose to teacher involvement in any other indirect areas.

A reader, applying the planning process to his own school situation, would probably find many infractions which may indicate that the planning process has never been employed and that, basically, planning for the improvement of instruction has not taken place. For example, the appraisal of plans, the last factor in the process, is seldom used by an individual teacher, a teaching team, or a system-wide committee—each concerned with the improvement of teaching-learning situations. Certainly there must be reasons for this; but, in many instances, we believe that originally very little, if any, thought was given to an appraisal of the initial plan since this is not the typical way we operate in public education. For planning to succeed, though, any staff member, whether he act as an individual or as a member of a group, should develop the habits of systematic introspection necessary to re-examine the most common of areas about which we improve the curriculum—the development of the teaching-learning situation. If we find no realistic planning in this most common area, then we can expect less planning in all other areas.

This first area for curriculum improvement has a unique aspect which should be mentioned. It is the one area of those diagrammed which employs the planning process for either an individual staff member developing plans related to one small aspect of a single learning situation, or for a group generating plans for a series of teaching-learning situations. One teacher might plan a single specific instructional objective for one pupil in an independent study situation. To do this, he would employ all aspects of the planning process. A representative system-wide committee of social studies teachers might plan a resource unit, and they would use all aspects of the planning process. In both cases, one should notice the following: (1) involvement of staff members in the development of plans, especially the involvement of those who have the responsibility to execute the plans, (2) reliance on authoritative background information, (3) development and execution of plans, and (4) appraisal of the action patterns which are the result of planning.

Perhaps our greatest fault in curriculum development is the failure to recognize the importance of the factors involved in the planning process at even this most common and minute of curriculum areas. If the use of these planning-factors is sloughed off at this level, think how easily they could be ignored during work at the pupil-teacher level, the system-wide level, or the state-wide level.

As we mentioned earlier, any planning done in this area relates directly to the decisions that classroom teachers make as they implement plans and translate plans into action. The plans made will be used by the teacher as he works with students. As a result, teachers need to be directly involved in the planning. Obviously, in this aspect of curriculum development, it is easy to recognize the need for teacher involvement. In fact, in matters that deal with the planning of unit topics objectives, content, materials, methodologies, or measuring devices, noninvolvement of teachers seems strange indeed although such noninvolvement is common.

2. *Improving the scope and sequence of learning activities; reporting pupil progress; physical facilities; and school organization. (Areas which are indirectly related to instruction.)* A study of the areas for curriculum improvement where planning does not directly influence classroom work may lead one to suppose that, within these areas, teacher involvement may be desirable but not necessary. This supposition is incorrect. Even in these curricular areas where the planned improvements are indirectly related to the classroom work of the teacher, the involvement of the total staff—teachers included—is necessary. Typically, in many school systems, teachers are not involved in planning in areas such as scope and sequence, physical facilities, and the like which indirectly influence curriculum improvement. But this cannot persist. For reasons indicated in the preceding chapter, teachers need to be involved in curriculum planning; and, if teachers need to be involved in planning because they represent a vital force, then their role in studying these indirect areas must be encouraged by the supportive staff and made obligatory by the teacher himself. Perhaps normally busy people shy away from such activities. However, if the planning process is to be used to improve the curriculum of a school, a teacher, as well as any staff member, has no alternative but to involve himself in planning areas which influence his work. Also, an administrator, or any other supportive staff member, has a responsibility to aid the teacher to perform a direct role in this planning. We seek the improvement of instruction; and, to that end, indirect areas for study will probably be best identified by the total staff, or its representatives, meeting to plan courses of action which can be subjected to the factors described in the planning process.

The areas listed in this section of the diagram are only illustrative of many areas which staffs have identified or tagged for improvement. Others which might have been listed are: developing insights for working with the mentally retarded (as well as other areas involving exceptional children), developing research programs, identifying in-service activities, developing programs to explore the uses of innovations, or studying the characteristics of the young adolescent. All these examples have one element in common: they require a system-wide planning attack. The participants have one overriding purpose: to define a set of specific plans which wil be helpful to the teaching staff, helpful in the sense that the plans will provide a sense of direction in the selection of specific teaching-learning situations. In other words, the potential of the classroom teacher cannot reach maximum efficiency unless prior plans aid in the development of classroom decisions. But, again, when not all factors of the planning process have been employed, many mistakes are made. For example, new buildings have been designed and old buildings have been modified without total staff involvement or authoritative background. Such physical facilities are a disgrace to modern education. Curriculum guides have been developed and printed without ever being used or appraised after use—if they were used at all. New, but useless, scope and sequence patterns of organization have been put into effect without staff participation in the development, without using authoritative sources, and without follow-up appraisal, This type of activity, which is not planning, has generated numerous problems which have frustrated teachers. All kinds of combinations of the factors in planning have been ignored. Therefore, planning has not taken place.

Unless there is a concerted effort by teachers and other professional staff members to use the planning process, the ineffective work in these areas is easily recognizable. The responsibility lies with teachers and other staff members to perform a lively role in the development of action patterns no matter what their degree of relationship to the learning of children or adults. If teachers need more time to participate, this need must be made known to the administration in order that proper scheduling can be done. If an administrator needs more time because of numerous duties, his needs must be made known to the board of education. The process of planning for improved education is too important to be for any reason set aside.

Improved Teaching-Learning Situations for Students

Reaching this stage in the sequence of curriculum planning activities does not signal the end. One cannot relax. This box on the diagram represents both a static condition and the culmination of a series of moves to improve that which had existed in the past. This box represents the new *status quo* which now serves as the basis for further examination in order to identify new problems, new ideals, interests, or needs. This is why the arrow on the diagram directs the eye back to the top of the page.

What one does regarding this area is similar to what one does for the first area, which discussed the identification of problems and the like. Beyond that, this area encourages an appraisal of final plans. The suggested behavior at this stage of curriculum development should be to observe what exists against an overlay of ideals defined in the past. Have the ideals been reached? Has the school staff closed the gap between what exists and those ideals? Have action patterns been taken to solve problems which caused the original planning?

At this stage, a sophisticated sense of planning must persist because at precisely this stage a typical school staff may relax. Perhaps this is natural since a difficult task is finished, the job is done, or the problem solved. But curriculum development cannot stop! We are not advocating change for the sake of change. We are, instead, asking planners to be aware of a tendency to believe that the solution to a problem eliminates the need to think of further related problems when, in reality, an excellent solution may cause numerous other problems. No period of rest can be found. A pseudo sense of respite may develop, but this feeling can be set aside by a staff aware of the process of continuous appraisal. Such appraisal identifies new problems and needs which are created by action patterns designed to meet prior situations. The examples are numerous. The elementary school staff, after deciding to follow the philosophy of the nongraded school, soon discovers that new needs arise in the areas of flexible building facilities and varied instructional materials, to mention but two items. The secondary school staff, after planning to use modular scheduling and place emphasis on the individualization of instruction through independent study and small group procedures, discovers rapidly that the distinct problem of planning time for teachers demands priority for solution. Much evidence suggests the belief that the process of continuous curriculum development can never be slowed.

Finally, at this stage, a danger exists which overshadows the others. Conceivably, the action pattern taken to improve the curriculum for a group of students may destroy the means whereby the staff achieved the original action pattern. This happens when the staff, inadvertently, adopts an end which discontinues further use of the means used to achieve the end. This means-ends relationship cannot be broken without destroying the entire planning process. If, for example, because of original poor planning, a group of elementary school teachers decided to solve a scope-and-sequence problem by adopting a solution which required all teachers to conduct learning experiences within the confines of the school, no community-centered activities could be allowed, since such would now "disrupt the normal operations" of a school. This solution would limit the planning that could be done in regard to the use of community-service projects. This action pattern would destroy any promise of further thought being given to community activities of this variety. A school staff must be quick to notice the inherent danger in such a move. It could effectively cut off further discussion and planning, both means which might solve a very real and contemporary problem in community-centered education. This is a very important point, and more will be said about it in the last chapter of this book.

In this review of the two-page diagram, we have stressed that the four factors of the planning process permeate all aspects of curriculum development. To that end, we have shown curriculum development to be a process whereby the total school staff assumes major responsibility to study the instructional program, to solve the problems that exist, to meet the instructional needs and interests that are discovered, and to check the results against the ideals. We have emphasized, again and again, a continuous process which demands teacher involvement not only in areas directly affecting their classroom work but also in areas indirectly affecting their classroom work. The outcome of such planning is the development, execution, and appraisal of specific procedures to improve the curriculum of the school for the learner. We have placed the highest priority of emphasis on planning for the improvement of instruction. Perhaps this topic should be developed further to indicate the difference that exists between the purpose of teacher involvement in planning and the purpose of in-service education for teachers.

PLACING THE EMPHASIS ON PLANNING THE IMPROVEMENT OF INSTRUCTION

At the risk of developing another "academic" point regarding the differences which seem to exist between what has been said about *planning* and the tack taken by many school administrators today, the following points need re-emphasis. The concept of curriculum planning advocated places major emphasis on the imrovement of teaching-learning situations for students as a result of scientific and cooperative planning or intelligent decision making by teachers. A concomitant of such planning may be the individual professional growth of the teachers and administrative staff members. At this time in the history of professional edcation, this concept of planning and decision making indicates that the major purpose of this professional effort is to improve instruction. However, this belief does not necessarily describe many ongoing conditions in educational circles today. In fact, many writers do not advocate this point of view in the field of educational administration, supervision, and curriculum development. On the contrary, their point of view, briefly stated, is that teachers' professional growth through *in-service education* shall be the prime purpose of curriculum planning activities. A concomitant of in-service "training" will be the improvement of the instructional program.

Spears has especially emphasized this point of view. He writes:

> It is fair enough to conclude that the in-service training program blankets—in the other two, curriculum planning and

supervision; it represents the entire organized effort of a school system to assure teachers' growth on the job. For its activity, its things to do, it draws especially upon the improvement of the instructional program—curriculum planning. Since much of the time of supervisors is directed toward the same goal, the in-service movement has likewise commandeered the effort of supervision.[5]

Philosophically speaking, what point of view should be emphasized in order to improve instruction? The point of everything written here, in contrast with what Harold Spears and others have written, is that the *planning* point of view must be emphasized because the end goal is the improvement of instruction. Curriculum planning, *per se,* gets at this task, first. In-service education, on the other hand, is basically concerned with the professional growth of the individual teacher. Perhaps in reality this does not make much difference since the "end" goal is always the same: the improvement of teaching-learning situations for the pupils. However, emphasis might make a difference.

Planning emphasizes that the entire staff (administrators and teachers) focus their thinking on the cooperative venture of creating a better environment for learning. The teacher in this context is considered a vital link in the chain of suggested improvements. The teacher is considered a professional worker who has enthusiasm, knowledge, and a sense of obligation to improve an instructional program. The superintendent, principal, supervisor, or curriculum worker recognizes the professional competencies of his teaching staff and also recognizes the task he faces—to help these people carry out this professional obligation. His (the administrator's) task is to know their needs, provide experts when needed, encourage the group process, and help the teachers to develop plans. Together, the total staff carries out its primary mission: improving the instructional program. Is in-service education ignored? Not at all. The professional teacher, as a result of his concern for the improvement of instruction, recognizes distinct lacks in his knowledge, ability, and understanding. He reaches a point,

---

[5] Harold Spears, *Curriculum Planning Through In-Service Programs* (Englewood Cliffs, N.J.: Prentice-Hall, Inc., 1957), pp. 43–44.

again as the result of involvement in planning activities, where he gets to know himself. He has the opportunity to recognize his deficiencies. He, or the administrator, then makes arrangements for in-service education activities which have as their primary aim the professional growth of that individual teacher —professional growth related to needs that he (the teacher) feels because he is incapable, without in-service education activities, of making a further contribution to the welfare of curriculum-planning activities.

In all this there is no coercion to have the teacher "get" some in-service "training." The administrator or supervisor does not "push" the teacher into a specific in-service activity. Teachers do not have to be "whipped" into shape. This may have been the case as far back as 1926 when administrators and supervisors were warned about the "training" of teachers.

> In the degree that curriculum making disregards the training of teachers it will be ineffective. If no provision is made for training teachers in the use of a changed or revised course of study, the old program is almost certain to persist. Changes made on paper remain on paper until they are translated into the habits and abilities of teachers.[6]

The implications we read into this may be erroneous, but a further perusal of this chapter will indicate that curriculum "making" would be done by the experts, and then the classroom teachers would be led to in-service activities which would help them to teach the new or revised course of study.

More modern texts on educational administration and supervision also emphasize that an important task of the "educational leader" is to "encourage" in-service activities for his staff.

In their chapter on the "Administrator and the Curriculum," Anderson and Davies write:

> In assuming his continuing responsibility to improve the curriculum, the realistic administrator normally anticipates a certain amount of staff resistance to new methods and ideas. The

---

[6] National Society for the Study of Education, *Twenty-Sixth Yearbook, Part I, The Foundations and Technique of Curriculum-Making: Curriculum-Making: Past and Present* (Bloomington, Ill.: Public School Publishing Company, 1926), p. 160.

desire of many faculty members to cling to traditional methods of work poses a challenge to his leadership, initiative, and ingenuity. He must transform complacency and lethargy into creativeness and activity to make his faculty a working team for the improvement of the educational program.

Inspirational leadership and the ability to stimulate activity are basic requirements of the administrator in marshaling the energies of his staff. While these qualities are indispensable and should operate at all times, the administrator should crystallize his efforts to train the staff by developing an organized program of in-service education.[7]

Surely, if the concern of professional educators today is for the improvement of the profession and the professional worker, a fresh and different concept must be advocated toward the classroom teacher. It is highly questionable whether or not a concept should be advocated whereby a school administrator should anticipate a certain amount of "staff resistance"; it is subject to doubt that many teachers desire to "cling to traditional methods." The words and ideas smack of unprofessionalism. The belief seems to be that unwilling and stupid workers in education must be lead by an enlightened, benevolent administrator before there can be professionalism in the ranks. If this were the case, then in-service education activities would deserve to be considered of prime importance. But what comes after in-service education—after the staff has achieved certain professional competencies? Does the administrator then decide that planning the improvement of the educational program is of prime importance? Does he then decide that the teachers are professional, and that they can become involved in cooperative planning in order that they might identify their own incompetencies? If this were the end goal, there would be no need to worry about the future of curriculum planning and improved teacher-decision-making.

Perhaps pupil-teacher planning, advocated and used for years and years, can help explain the primary need for teacher involvement in curriculum planning while in-service activities should take a "back seat." Involving the pupil in certain types of learning environments leads to a build-up of certain needs,

---

[7] Vivienne Anderson and Daniel R. Davies, *Patterns of Educational Leadership* (Englewood Cliffs, N.J.: Prentice-Hall, Inc., 1956), p. 42.

interests, wants, and desires. These needs, and the like, help the teacher and the pupil to evolve purposes for study, for learning, and for self-directed, meaningful activity. The child lives life and learns to become a "professional" human being who interacts with his environment. He experiences, and he goes on and on to live a rich life of continuous education. The teacher is the guide. The teacher directs this interaction, this experience, this "mulling-over" process we call education. He helps the child to develop habits of learning that enable him (the child) to be a student the remainder of his life whether he is in the systematic school situation or not.

Can we picture the same condition for the teacher? Through curriculum-planning activities (which need extremely careful thinking through by the administrative staff), can we involve teachers in an environment of curricular problems, interests, and the like? Can we give teachers the task to improve, continuously and cooperatively, the educational program? This can be done; and, where it has been done, where it has been the prime purpose of curriculum planning, needs (and desires, interests, and wants) are created in the professional teacher. In-service education will result because the teacher feels the need. There is no earthly reason in the mind of this teacher to cling to traditional methods, to throw up a resistance to change, or to need an administrator to transform him from a complacent and lethargic worker into a creative and imaginative one. The entire concept would be ridiculous, and the concept is truly ridiculous where curriculum planning is the prime objective for a local school staff. In situations where curriculum planning exists, no administrator has to marshal the energies of his staff. Instead he must marshal his own energies to administer the innovations his staff makes.

We question whether the concept of individual professional growth of the teacher is needed today as a prime way in which to improve the instructional program. Instead, the prime professional emphasis must be on the cooperative, systematic improvement of teaching-learning experiences for pupils in our schools. We question whether the administrator today should challenge his "lethargic" staff into in-service educational activities in order to improve the educational program. Instead, the administrator today must "administer" his staff's educational programs which result from their involvement in curriculum planning.

Administrators and supervisors need to consider, more and more, what it means to work with expert teachers. In curriculum planning, a striking danger exists that the administrative staff will persist in emphasizing in-service education for well-educated teachers as the fundamental purpose of planning. Perhaps these teachers disagree with this purpose and find the entire point of view degrading.

To the professional teacher, the prime purpose of curriculum planning is the identification and solution of instructional problems. These teachers feel a responsibility to make decisions about the all-school program; they feel that they are experts in deciding how to direct and guide pupils through various phases of an educational program.

In terms of the teachers' workaday world, the immediate and related classroom instructional problems and their solution are of prime importance. In-service education (individual professional growth) comes second. It is possible that any attempt by the administrative staff to persist in this "in-service" viewpoint when working with teachers concerned with curriculum planning may create a Frankenstein monster whose personality might be warped by feelings of confusion, low morale, cynicism, or, worst of all, indifference.

SUMMARY

The process of planning, if understood and practiced by all school staff members, serves as the atmosphere in which teacher decision-making may well be facilitated. This process, defined and practiced, may lead school staffs to find ways to improve the school program—ways which have never been dreamed of before. Involvement of professional staff workers in planning may mean that enough instructional problems will be defined and solved to place education on a scientific plateau. Decision making, then, on the level of classroom operation, may become the scientific work which it could become and which it has already become in many localities.

Involvement of teachers in planning should mean that the process will be used to improve teaching-learning situations for pupils. Teachers are not involved in planning for purposes of in-service education. A teacher's involvement in in-service education should be the result of a decision he makes after he recognizes his own deficiences in curriculum planning.

Finally, cooperative planning by school staffs should result in decision making on an echelon higher than that on which the individual teacher operates in the classroom. Perhaps it follows that such cooperative planning, with its concomitant decisions, may improve the role of the individual teacher. Over-all curriculum planning may help the individual teacher be more professional and make more intelligent decisions. In like manner, curriculum planning and teacher involvement in such planning may lead to a definition of teachers' needs and responsibilities. Satisfying these needs and helping teachers meet their responsibilities is the task of the administrator in public education.

CHAPTER FOUR

THE TEACHER—HIS NEEDS

The relaxed but sincere atmosphere of the "bull session" would encourage a discussion of the topic: "Should the teacher be an artist or a scientific worker?" In this chapter we do not intend to argue that question. Instead, we want to speculate about those tangible and intangible factors which influence the curriculum-planning activities of a classroom teacher. We will assume that the classroom teacher has an obligation to make value judgments about the education of pupils—value judgments which stem from a critical and reflective analysis of evidence and theory about instructional programs. When the teacher does this, we think he is being professional in his behavior. This professional behavior we identify as necessary for educational planning. This behavior, certainly, is scientific. Now, if the teacher carries out his obligation and has, therefore, a scientific attitude, what factors should be analyzed which may help the scientific teacher meet his obligation and make a distinct contribution to the planning concept?

The American public school teacher who makes decisions feels a host of unmet needs as he tries to be professional. These needs range from academic freedom to in-service educational opportunities. Our purpose is to try to identify and discuss those needs and interests which are intimately related to successful curriculum-planning activities. Heaven knows the typical public school teacher seeks economic security in various forms, as well as other advantages which promote feelings of status and belongingness within the community.

But these areas will not be treated here. Instead we are concerned with those needs and interests related to the improvement of instruction. The first important area is the freedom of the teacher to teach.

FREEDOM TO TEACH (ACADEMIC FREEDOM)

An examination of the term *academic freedom* is necessary. At times this valuable concept has been defined and explained in such a way that the public school teacher, because of his lack of expert subject-matter-area authority, has been left high and dry—out of the swim of things. Therefore, some definitions of academic freedom preclude the role of the public school teacher. Writers, such as Howard Mumford Jones, have ignored the teachers in the American public school systems because they "are locally controlled, and local politics can on occasion be a grave threat to honest teaching."[1] Community and administrative control limit and, at times, destroy the individual's freedom to teach, freedom to do research, and freedom related to his community activity. (Therefore, the public school teachers' tasks are not considered within the realm of academic freedom.) But whatever the definitions, the typical concepts contain basic elements related to the teachers' free search for truth and the free exposition of this truth.

Unfortunately, perhaps because of the lack of clarity of a definition of "expert authority" and because of a misinterpretation and confusion of terms such as "local control," "free search," and "free exposition," the academic-freedom needs of the public school teacher have been unceremoniously pushed aside. Nevertheless, each elementary school teacher or high school teacher does need and want academic freedom. His professional teacher-decision-making activities depend on it, and his role as a curriculum planner requires it. Basic questions need to be asked. In what areas does the community exercise control? In what areas should the teacher exercise control? Finally, what does freedom to teach really mean to the teacher trying desperately to make professional decisions?

---

[1] Howard Mumford Jones, "The American Concept of Academic Freedom," *AAUP Bulletin,* XLVI (March 1960), 66–72.

Academic freedom means that the public school teacher is an expert. One of the accepted earmarks of a professional person is his ability to use his education and experience to make critical judgments or choices regarding problem situations that arise. The physicist may make judgments regarding the specific field of research that must be studied in relation to radiation effects on the human body,[2] the dentist makes judgments regarding the repair of a dental cary, and a physician employs his knowledge to diagnose an illness. Each professional faces a problem situation requiring a solution or action pattern. Decisions are required. The individual involved cannot "pass the buck." The problem ends with him. His ability to suggest and try the "best" course of action depends on his knowledge, experience, creative ability, and freedom to make decisions in light of the values held by himself and the community.

The teacher, the curriculum planner, also makes hundreds of decisions a day and is controlled by similar factors. Within the teaching-learning situations he must direct, he is constantly forced to make critical judgments and choices. There are five basic frames of reference in which he makes these decisions. These five areas encompass most of his workaday world; and, contrary to what some authors may write, teachers do make decisions in these areas everyday. These areas are:

1. The definition of specific instructional objectives.
2. The choice and organization of subject-matter items or centers of interest.
3. The choice of classroom activities or techniques.
4. The choice of instructional materials.
5. The determination of student progress in direct relation to the statement of instructional objectives.

Obviously, the opportunity to "define," "choose," and "determine" is tremendously influenced and limited by community and administrative controls, but not as much as some writers would lead us to believe. Probably the greatest factor which

---

[2] Harold K. Schilling, "Physics as Decision Making," *Illinois State University Journal*, XXVIII (September 1965), 7–21.

has limited the decision-making activities of public school teachers has been the lack of knowledge about the areas we have listed. This same limiting factor could be related to the college professor (teacher and researcher) who, although he believes he has freedom to teach and freedom to pursue research, nevertheless is hidebound by his lack of ability to define his teaching goals, the subject matter best suited for these goals, as well as the classroom or laboratory methods and materials necessary to get the task done. In like manner, the researcher is limited by his inability to define significant problems and follow through with the best research methods to solve his problems.

Basically, then, if the public school teacher may be classified as an expert, it is within these areas:

1. *The definition of specific instruction objectives for an individual or a group of pupils.* This task challenges the teacher. The challenge may be unmet, and the result may be fuzzy thinking about the most important area of "expertness" the teacher tries to attain. The task of defining goals may loom so large that the teacher is overcome with feelings of frustration, and the inability to define goals limits the ability of the teacher to conduct the teaching-learning experience. More important, such limitations influence his ability to define his academic freedom, especially as that academic freedom is related to the freedom to teach.

Challenging as this task might be, the teacher must define goals, Failure to define them means aimless wandering through a maze of educational experiences. Such resultant accidental-incidental learning is expensive and inefficient. Tremendous sums of money allocated for the education of youth cannot be wasted by aimless wandering which may result from a lack of definition of the individual teacher's task in the classroom.

At the present time, university professors and public school teachers seem to have little trouble defining objectives concerned with basic skills or information. The elementary school teacher can define the arithmetic skills he intends to teach to a group over a given period of time. In like manner, a history professor can outline the information to be taught in English history. A swimming coach knows what specific skills he wants to teach. In most instances, there is little doubt about the specific instructional objectives within these areas. However, the types of objectives that might be taught go beyond the mere acquisition of skills and information.[3] Hence, the inability to define all types of objectives limits the expertness of the teacher and his academic freedom. Inability to define specific understandings, for example, seriously impedes an educational program. In other words, the inability to define specific instructional objectives related to teaching understandings, or related to the ability of the student to utilize knowledge in some way, points up the inexpertness of the teacher. The same point can be made regarding the definition of goals related to teaching attitudes, appreciations, and the stimulation of interests.

Most teachers have been asked: "What are you trying to teach?" This question is difficult, especially when there is little time to prepare an answer. In fact, many times the person to whom the question is put becomes antagonistic toward the questioner. Some teachers believe that such questions are impertinent, and that the interviewer has no right to ask the question. Perhaps such feelings of antagonism toward the interviewer indicate frustrations which the teacher feels. Perhaps he is frustrated because he cannot answer the question except in vague generalities. Perhaps this teacher does not know, specifically, what he is trying to teach. Another teacher, when given the opportunity to prepare a workable set of instructional goals, responds in an altogether different manner when asked the same question. Confidently, he explains, in detail, where he intends to go with a group of students. He is not "out to see the sights"; he knows what "sights" he wants to see. If one challenge his "right" to teach "something," he knows the specific area about which is being challenged. Because this teacher is expert in defining goals or objectives, he has a knowledgeable grip on academic freedom. He is, in reality, an expert

---

[3] *Taxonomy of Educational Objectives, The Classification of Educational Goals, Handbook I: Cognitive Domain,* ed. Benjamin S. Bloom (New York: David McKay Company, Inc., 1956); and David R. Krathwohl, Benjamin S. Bloom and Bertram B. Masia, *Taxonomy of Educational Objectives, the Classification of Education Goals, Handbook II: Affective Domain* (New York: David McKay Company, Inc., 1956).

authority. He is professional. He makes judgments in his work which no one else can make.

It is necessary to remember at this point that we are discussing specific instructional objectives: those detailed goals or purposes which teachers (and sometimes students) define to accomplish the "over-all objectives" of the school. In this section our purpose is to emphasize the expert qualities needed by the teacher to guarantee gaining, controlling, and keeping academic freedom—a need of the scientific teacher interested in curriculum planning.

But what about academic freedom as it relates to the development of over-all objectives of an educational program? Legally, the people of a community through their elected Board of Education control the basic objectives of the school's program. This power is given to the community by the state. However, a mere summation of the legal control of public elementary and secondary schools does, in no way, eliminate the confusion of controls and the confusion of concepts about controls. In practice, the range of confusion is greatest because of the unique and distinct personality of each school district. Each pressure group (civic, social, religious, recreational, or economic), individual administrator, individual teacher, specific teachers' group, etc., has an ax to grind regarding what should be taught in the schools. Because of this confusion, many teachers are, in reality, the single controlling force because the objectives have never been spelled out by the conflicting groups. Also, in some subject-matter areas, the knowledgeable teacher has unlimited control of objectives because the laymen have not been able to keep up to date in those areas. They, the laymen, have relinquished control by default.

Today, although this confusion exists, two points seem to emerge. First, the community people need to redefine the basic task or purposes of the school; and, second, the teachers want the freedom to accomplish these objectives.

Does the community's definition of basic goals destroy the freedom the teacher seeks? Actually this question seems academic because, for the decision-making teacher, the destruction of academic freedom occurs when the community does *not* define the basic goals of education. In other words, the teacher finds it impossible to be professional when the basic tasks of the school are not clearly expressed. The teacher has to face questions such as these: How does one plan specific teaching-learning situations when the ultimate purpose has never been clearly defined? What is it the community wants us to do? What is the destination in regard to the education of the youth of a community or a state? Since public education is public, since it serves the needs of the public, since it is related to what the people of a community want for their children, the teacher cannot conduct his professional activities with any scientific flair until the cloud of confusion regarding the over-all task of the school is lifted.

To help the community people define the task of public education a host of activities and recommendations have been made. These recommendations have been made by professional educators and by citizens' groups. Contrary to what some people may think, the greatest number of suggestions of activities to help a community define the goals have come from the professionals in public education who recognize the need to accomplish this job.[4] They recognize that confusion of purpose is a basic threat to professional teaching. Citizens' groups also recognize that the lack of public interest means a lack of clear definition of purpose and a weakening of the school structure itself.[5]

We are saying that the laymen must define the over-all task or function of the school. Only then can the teacher, or the staff of teachers, define the specific instructional objectives which will, in the long run, accomplish the over-all objectives which were defined by the people of the community. The teacher states specific instructional objectives and plans the teaching-learning experiences for pupils. He cannot state these smaller objectives when there is confusion regarding the larger ones. For example, laymen have been bickering for decades about teaching sex education. Confusion exists in laymen's

---

[4] Such is established in numerous publications of the National Education Association.

[5] See: *Committee for the White House Conference on Education— Report to the President* (Washington, D.C.: U.S. Government Printing Office, 1956).

minds regarding this area as a *bona fide* objective for the school. There is no clear mandate from the public as there is regarding the teaching of reading, arithmetic, or citizenship. Hence, when the subject of sex or reproduction arises in a classroom situation, as it invariably does in a host of subject-matter areas, the teacher's action pattern for this teaching-learning situation is blurred and fuzzy. There are many similar examples in the areas of social problems, recreational activities, spiritual, moral, and ethical values, politics, economics, and on and on. The list is endless.

The public school teacher needs a clear statement of the purpose of the school if he is to be free to teach. Contrary, again, to what some authors say about community control of public education and how this eliminates the academic freedom of the teacher, to the practicing public school teacher the real threat to the freedom to teach lies in the confusion of basic school objectives. The public school teacher believes in public schools and the need for public participation in the definition of objectives. He does not fear community control; he fears the lack of community participation.

This is not to say, however, that the public school teacher encourages the laymen to tell him *how* to teach Johnny to read. At this point the teacher "backs away" from the laymen, but not too hastily since he realizes that laymen find it difficult to separate goals from methodology. Because it is difficult to separate the goal from the means to get there, the educator has the responsibility to help the laymen center their thinking on the task of the school; and once this has been done, the laymen will have less interest in the mechanics of the job.

To some readers, the above analysis may indicate that the public school teacher has little interest in academic freedom, that he has relinquished his rights to the laymen for whom the public schools exist, and that, once the purposes of the educational program have been defined, the teacher becomes a lackey whose only job is to do the master's bidding. Such an interpretation could be made. The public school teacher does have a specific task to perform, if that task is clearly defined. Still, even within this framework, the teacher wishes and needs professional autonomy in order to be able to carry out the task assigned to him. The teacher wishes and needs what Howard Mumford Jones labels 'the freedom to teach': [6] a freedom for the teacher to analyze the over-all objectives of an educational program so that he may clearly state the specific goals he must teach. Freedom to teach is necessary for the further definition of the subject matter, the instructional activities, and the instructional materials. This encompasses the sphere in which the public school teacher seeks and needs professional autonomy—an autonomy which "has been undermined, perhaps unwittingly, by some well-known figures in higher education."[7]

2. *The choice of subject matter or centers of interest.* When such a choice is made by the public school teacher, it indicates, again, an "expert authority" ability which qualifies him for academic freedom. Again, questions must be asked: Does the teacher really choose the subject matter to be taught? How much judgment is involved? How can we classify the teacher as an expert in this area?

Once the specific instructional objectives for a day's work or for a six-week's period have been determined, the teacher must define and organize the subject-matter content which will serve as a vehicle for accomplishing the objectives. No class can be taught without subject matter. Students must talk, read, write, discuss, do, make, or watch *something*. That something *is* the subject matter. In a second grade class, the subject matter for the next four weeks may be *Aviation*. Everything about this subject will serve as a center of interest or a point of departure as the teacher works with the students to help them accomplish specific goals which are related to arithmetic, language arts, science, history, and the like. The subject matter of a tenth grade biology class may be the community, with its wild life, water supply, and sewage disposal. In this case the specific goals concern themselves with learning information, gaining understandings, and utilizing scientific methods related to the general area of biology. There are many other examples that could be given, but the basic point holds: the

---

[6] Howard Mumford Jones, *op. cit.*
[7] Myron Lieberman, *Education as a Profession* (Englewood Cliffs, N.J.: Prentice-Hall, Inc., 1956), p. 116.

teacher had to make a judgment about the specific subject-matter content that could best accomplish the learning goals.

These judgments regarding subject matter do not spring full-blown from the head of Zeus. To the professional scientific teacher, the choice of subject matter is not incidental or accidental. Such decisions result from careful thinking about the best vehicle for the teaching-learning situations. Such thinking revolves about many criteria which, when woven together, make, for the teacher, a screen of selection. As criteria, the objectives are of first importance. Beyond this, and directly related to the objectives, are such criteria as curricular approaches, the scope and sequence of a series of learning experiences, the characteristics of the learner, and the classroom methods and instructional materials at the disposal of the teacher to mention but a few. Knowledge about these items enables the teacher to make critical judgments in choosing the subject matter for a class. Lack of knowledge about these areas obviously strips away the expert authority of the teacher. Then, the teacher cannot qualify for academic freedom.

There are cases where teachers cannot be professional because judgments regarding the organization of subject matter are impossible to make. The teacher follows the dictates of a textbook or a narrow course of study unrelated to different types of specific goals; the "tail"—subject matter, *per se*, wags the "dog"—the teaching-learning situation in the classroom. Then a well-defined body of knowledge becomes the end. Little thought is given to the purposes of the course of instruction except, perhaps, a purpose that the students should pass an examination. But, even here, the examination is not related to a specific objective, except perhaps, on the student's part, to get a "high" grade. Even here, the grade is not related to anything meaningful; and it, too, becomes an end in itself. The resultant vicious circle leads to stereotyped teaching which cannot be classified as professional. Certainly the people of a community, viewing this procedure, or having actually lived through this stereotyped performance, would not want to give to the teachers the gold coin of academic freedom.

3. *The choice of classroom methods or techniques.* This area also requires expert knowledge in order to make valid judgments about teaching-learning situations. As in the other areas, many public school teachers are competent in choosing and using teaching techniques and need freedom in this area in order to be professional. Each day, as a teacher preplans, he makes decisions about teaching methods. Since classroom methodology is important and vital to the development of teaching-learning situations, teachers have no alternative but to be expert, to make choices from the alternatives available, and to seek the academic freedom necessary for employing the proper methods.

Therefore, the teacher must know many techniques. Lecture, telling, reading aloud, small and large group discussions, pupil-teacher planning, recitation, committee activities, drill, problem solving, and laboratory activities indicate some methods which teachers employ in their workaday world. How does one know which method to use? The answer, of course, depends on the knowledge and experience of the teacher as well as his ability to consider specific purposes, pupils' characteristics, subject matter, and the availability of instructional materials. In the main, however, the immediate decision depends on his knowledge of the techniques themselves. Should the lecture, for example, be used to teach a skill such as bowling? The answer is obvious. Teachers should know automatically that there are specific reasons why a lecture should be used. The lecture has specific advantages, and it has disadvantages. In order to use it effectively, one must prepare in a certain way. There are pitfalls into which the inexperienced lecturer may fall. These and other points can be made not only in regard to the lecture, but also in relationship to pupil-teacher planning techniques as well as other techniques. Still, knowing teaching methodology is one thing; having the freedom to employ it is another thing.

4. *The choice of instructional materials.* Related to the decisions that are made about classroom methods are the decisions that are made about classroom instructional materials. The two go hand-in-hand. High ability is required in this area, and most public school teachers can be classified as experts about instructional materials. Nevertheless, the average teacher in

public schools still would like more freedom to choose the proper materials for his pupils.

Again, as with methods and techniques, the types of instructional materials are many. Some are: textbooks, supplementary books (as well as the wide range of other printed matter), laboratory equipment, charts, maps, chalkboards, audio-visual materials, and resource people and places. Again, the teacher decides which materials to use to accomplish the instructional goals. He chooses materials related to the subject matter, the pupils, and to the classroom technique to be employed. Again, he must ask himself the question: What are the advantages and limitations of the various types of materials? To answer the question he again uses a screen of selection which contain many criteria that he wishes he had more time to study.

The public school teacher is indeed an expert in the realm of choosing and using instructional materials. But new materials for pupils are developed every year, and the professional teacher cannot allow a lack of knowledge about new materials to destroy his opportunity and freedom to make decisions regarding their use.

5. The determination of student progress. This is the last area in which we believe that the teacher of today is trying to be expert and in which the teacher also feels that he must be free to make decisions that are based on expert knowledge. Determining student progress is, at best, unscientific. It is an area, somewhat as the others are, which the public school teacher is trying desperately to master. More and more he employs paper-pencil measuring devices, anecdotal evidence, interviews, rating scales, logs, and diaries to determine student progress in direct relation to the stated specific instructional objectives and/or behavioral criteria.

Here, again, the teacher feels the need to be free to use his expertness to choose the proper medium for measuring pupil progress. At the same time, the teacher feels the need to study these devices. Such freedom is slow in coming in areas where the Regents Examinations or special city-wide measuring devices are used. Such freedom is especially slow to come when the administration of a school system insists on an overabundance of paper-pencil type tests, or when colleges and universities require for admittance a grade on a measuring device which is narrow in scope.

Thus, whether the area of decision making relates to measuring student progress or to the other four areas we have been discussing, the public school teacher of today is knowledgeable and does employ the results of education and experience in making judgments. As far as knowledge goes, he is an expert in these areas. He needs to make decisions. He needs the freedom to make decisions.

Perhaps more space should be given to a more detailed analysis of this basic need of the scientific teacher. Perhaps it should be emphasized that most nonprofessionals think of academic freedom as related to the selection of subject matter or a body of knowledge to be learned by the pupils. Many writers refer to this as the "curriculum." Our purpose is to show that the scientific teacher goes beyond this concept of teaching and classroom management. He needs freedom to make decisions in the other areas we have mentioned as well. His needs for academic freedom in all these areas must be satisfied in order that he may decide, as an individual or in a group, the curriculum-planning activities necessary for the improvement of the instructional program.

TIME FOR TEACHER PREPLANNING

Somehow, the mistaken notion has evolved that, if a person knows his subject matter area very well, he can confidently stride into any classroom and teach. In the practical situation nothing is farther from the truth. Such a "teacher" may be lulled into the belief that, because he has presented the subject matter, he has taught something to somebody. But this mishmash of activity encourages sloppy thinking about the teacher's task. Unquestionably, the teacher needs time to plan many items for the work in the classroom. In all other professions the need for preplanning is recognized. Very few people would have a home built without giving the architect or the contractor time for planning. In fact, any construction or engineering job requires enormous preplanning sometime before the task is started. Air-line pilots would not attempt a flight without a careful plan—careful enough to predict, to the minute, the estimated time or arrival. Many such illustrations could be given in regard to surgery, trial law, preaching, or professional football. To believe that no preplanning time is required to teach is to assume that simple repetition will cause learning. Such automatic behavior belongs on the assembly line or inside the calculating machines, not in those situations which call for unique judgments.

Teaching requires unique judgments *before* the teaching-learning situation and *during* the teaching-learning situation. The latter is dependent on the former. The experienced teacher who can prepare carefully for the classroom situation can make competent spot judgments during the teaching situation. Perhaps we could say that the preplanning judgments a teacher makes are indicative of scientific behavior; and the classroom judgments are indications of artistic behavior. However, as was suggested earlier, this is an argument which we should set aside.

If the teacher seeks preplanning time, what does he think about? Very briefly, the following points could be listed:

1. The needs, interests, and characteristics of the learners.
2. The specific aims and objectives for the classroom session stated in relation to the over-all task of the school.
3. The specific group and individual classroom activities which will be used.
4. The subject-matter area, issue, or problem which will serve as the vehicle for accomplishing the objectives.
5. The wide variety of possible instructional materials such as printed matter, chalkboard, or audio-visual aids which might be used.
6. The possible measuring devices which could be used to identify student progress or achievement in terms of the specific objectives identified.

Obviously, there are further items that the teacher must consider if he has time. These items include homework, transition between today's lesson and tomorrow's lesson, the curricular approach to emphasize the physical facilities of the classroom and school, the time of day, the relationship of his lesson to the responsibilities of other teachers, the teacher's own competence, and many others. Literally, there are a hundred factors that cannot be ignored.

OPPORTUNITY FOR INDIVIDUAL PROFESSIONAL GROWTH

Just as the teacher needs time to plan, he needs the opportunity to acquire the substance of his decision making in the form of in-service educational opportunity. In other words, time alone will not satisfy his needs. There must be the opportunity to gain knowledge regarding the profession itself, but the definition of this need should grow out of involvement in curriculum planning.

This may seem an obvious point—one that should not be labored. After all, one could argue, numerous activities and opportunity for professional growth are already available. What more does the teacher need? In a way this is true; but sometimes a teacher can intellectually starve in the midst of plenty. State and national professional meetings are arranged to help teachers (although frequently very few can attend, the time element is too short, or the crowds are too great); professional journals provide information; and university courses in subject-matter areas and professional education seemingly leave little to be desired. Certainly, here is opportunity for individual professional growth. In these cases, however, the in-service activities are a step removed from the immediate instructional problems of the staff. Certainly, individual professional growth is necessary and desirable, but *opportunity* for growth must be related to the intimacy, immediacy, and relevancy of the local instructional problems. The opportunity for individual professional growth through in-service education is decidedly limited by the very nature of the format of the offerings; and, therefore, the bulk of teachers feel the need for greater opportunity in this area.

The three areas of in-service education mentioned above will undoubtedly retain their present format and, perhaps, rightly so. A sincere case could be made for professional writings, meetings, and classes which serve the general professional needs of teachers. No doubt such opportunities must be made available continuously. Such services may continue to provide general information which the teacher has to translate into useable knowledge for making classroom judgments. General articles and meetings devoted to subject-matter areas, the characteristics of children and culture, or the utilization of instructional methods and materials are increasingly helpful to the professional worker. However, there are intimate and immediate teacher instructional problems which require a different type of in-service education opportunity.

When these urgent needs arise, the general format of university classes, regional meetings, or national magazines serves no immediate purpose. The immediate development of an elementary school science program requires, instead, that an individual teacher grow professionally in an area which is not systematically outlined in any course of instruction, periodical, or national meeting. Now, opportunity for in-service education is needed within the school system itself. Many immediate instructional problems have resulted in many local in-service educational opportunities for the staff. This concept lead Spears to organize a book that "grew out of a desire to go into various school systems to see what they are doing in the way of in-service education of teachers and staff."[8] A moment later, he goes on to say: "The in-service movement is not necessarily an exciting subject; rather, it is an impressive one, because of the great number of teachers involved, the sincere intensity of their effort, and the wholesome promise of the thing."[9]

The "promise of the thing," we think, lies in the individual's professional growth that results when the staff has the opportunity to study areas related to local instructional problems which are relevant to the judgments a staff makes in the local school. Where few, if any, in-service educational activities exist that are related to local instructional problems, then local teachers have an unmet need which prevents them from assuming professional autonomy.

[8] Harold Spears, *Curriculum Planning Through In-Service Programs* (Englewood Cliffs, N.J.: Prentice-Hall, Inc., 1947), p. vii.
[9] *Ibid.,* p. vii.

IMPROVED COMMUNICATION AND ARTICULATION PROCEDURES

Not only do teachers interested in professional autonomy need time and opportunity for growth: they need procedures which will assure communications and articulation among and between themselves and other teachers and staff members. The education of a pupil is a cooperative affair. All too often the third-grade teacher, for example, has only meager evidence of what a second-grade teacher has tried to teach. Or, a home economics teacher has experienced certain frustrations while teaching family living to a ninth-grade class because specific audio-visual aids were already used with a majority of the class members in a core class. In like manner, one teacher of eleventh-grade United States History could benefit immensely by hearing, from other teachers of similar subject matter, about useful methods and materials in teaching a unit about the *U.S. Constitution*. Although much has been written to help overcome articulation difficulties in public education, such difficulties still exist. Although there are such difficulties between each grade level and subject-matter areas, the most significant barriers to communication still stand between primary and intermediate grade levels, intermediate and junior high school, junior high school and senior high school, and senior high and college.

Various procedures have been tried to increase communication and articulation. The most common procedure has been the simplest and probably the most significant: grouping teachers who share a common interest or instructional problem. Groups of teachers and staff members who share a common interest or problem forget their petty bickering as they enthusiastically explore solutions. During this process the concern for communication and articulation, *per se,* is lost in the ongoing activity of the group. Careful development of a cumulative record folder system as well as careful preparation of pupil progress systems assure, to some degree, communication about pupils and their progress through the school's grades. In any case, whatever the procedure attempted, the gain might overcome some of the distressing needs which teachers feel in this area. Improvement of communication and articulation between teachers and staff members certainly needs to be listed as an important factor to be satisfied before we can think seriously about the professional tasks of the teacher. A factor such as this one, once ignored, snares the total operation of teaching and prevents the teacher from making intelligent judgments about teaching-learning situations.

ASSISTANCE IN DECISION-MAKING AREAS

A teacher makes many decisions each day as he works with pupils. These decisions are the result of careful pre-service, in-service study, and curriculum planning. With the rapid advance of new professional knowledge, the teacher needs expert or consultant help in order to translate and utilize this knowledge. These areas of professional knowledge concern themselves with a study of (1) the learner, (2) the learning process, (3) instructional objectives, (4) the subject matter areas, (5) instructional materials, (6) instructional methods, and (7) measuring devices. The immediate need is to supply consultant help to aid in the utilization of the latest information about these areas. Such help could come from numerous sources. Often local public school people have expert knowledge which they have learned to use in these decision-making areas. They may be teachers who have done advanced study. They may be staff personnel such as principals, supervisors, curriculum workers, guidance workers, school psychologists, and the like. Nearby colleges and universities may have staff members particularly suited to help teachers. Help can also be found in the numerous books, pamphlets, and periodicals. Of course, the alert school administrator will provide help in making such resource people or materials available to the staff. In order to emphasize the content of the areas in which expert help is needed, each of the seven items listed in this paragraph will now be discussed briefly.

1. *The behavioral characteristics of the learner.* The nature of the learner perpetually concerns the teacher. He needs detailed knowledge about the learner's intellectual, social, emotional,

and physical characteristics. Beyond this the teacher needs knowledge about how the student reacts with his peers, how he thinks about himself (his self-perception), the developmental tasks he faces, and the special needs and interests he feels as he grows in his culture. *However, the basic teacher need regarding this area relates to utilizing this body of knowledge about the child. The teacher concerns himself not with a child,* per se, *but rather with the child as a learner in a teaching-learning situation.* To accomplish this the teacher needs more than the basic knowledge from the scientist who studies human behavior; the teacher needs more than the basic knowledge of society or the knowledge of the interplay between groups and individuals within the social scene. The contributions of the psychologists, sociologists, anthropologists, and the like, are vitally important; but nevertheless, the teacher needs help in translating their knowledge to the functional teaching-learning situation.

The teacher, by profession, works with the child as a learner. In other words, the teacher today needs functional knowledge about the learner in order to improve teaching-learning decisions. For example, how a pupil perceives himself and the role he might play as a worker in society certainly could influence teacher's decisions about the activities for that pupil as he studies a unit on "vocations." Or, the intellectual ability of a tenth grader could aid the language arts teacher in deciding the specific novel (instructional material) which the pupil could read to accomplish specific objectives.

Every year the amount of new information reported in this area is enormous. It is pleasant to report that this area is being studied diligently, and such functional knowledge will aid the teacher tremendously. However, it is depressing to report that the other six areas we are about to discuss are not receiving the same attention although the needs of the professional teacher in these areas are clear.

2. *The learning process.* In this area, any contributions which the learning psychologists can evolve will satisfy needs of the professional teacher. At the present time, the classroom worker recognizes the existence of various theories of learning and encourages the detailed studies that are being conducted and

reported. But the need is still unmet. The teacher recognizes that the learning process is a dynamic interaction between the learner and the environment and that this interaction is based on a host of experiential factors, but the teacher needs to know more. Today the teacher feels confident that he knows something of the learning process when the student learns simple information and skills. On the other hand, the teacher does not know what happens when he tries to teach under-standings, attitudes, appreciations, and interests to a group of students. Once the objective is stated, he does not know, for sure, what to do next to guarantee learning. When informa-tion about learning theories can be verified in the school and when this information, in turn, can serve as guideposts to the teacher who must make decisions, perhaps the feelings of frustrations which result from a lack of knowledge will be dispelled, and perhaps the teacher's need will be met.[10]

3. *Instructional objectives.* Untold chapters could be written about the confusion regarding the objectives of an instruc-tional program. This confusion needs to be unraveled for the teacher; or, better still, the teacher needs to know how to un-ravel it in order to make decisions about a specific educational program. Basically, we have two elements of confusion. The first relates to a distinct lack of clarity of basic goals of public education, and the second relates to continuity between basic goals and classroom purposes. The day-by-day classroom goals grow from the over-all goals that should be determined by the people of a community—local, state, or national. How can a professional teacher build a series of teaching-learning situ-ations when the basic end goal is not clearly defined, deline-ated, and detailed? But determination of specific goals (the task of the teacher) is not simple because their determination is affected by a host of factors such as curricular approaches, college preparatory education, honors, and grading systems, to mention a few. Such extraneous factors *should not* and *need not* influence the statement of purposes, but they do. When

---

10 National Society for the Study of Education, *Theories of Learning and Instruction, 63rd Yearbook, Part I,* ed. Ernest R. Hilgard (Chicago: The University of Chicago Press, 1964). See particularly Chapter XVII by Ernest R. Hilgard.

this haziness exists, when the foundation is shaky, the resultant wobbly superstructure is weakened and ready to topple.

Further help is needed in understanding what an objective means. For example, what does it mean to say that the specific objective of a lesson is "to understand" something, "to assimilate" something, "to appreciate" something, "to develop an attitude toward" something, or "to think critically about" something? Such objectives are really confusing to teachers although such objectives are consistently stated by teachers. And the accomplishment of these objectives is even more difficult. How does the teacher translate these statements into measurable classroom, school, or community behavior? To further describe this area of confusion, the teacher must ask himself other seemingly unanswerable questions: What objectives did the preceding teacher try to accomplish? What success, if any, did he have? Is there any specific evidence that any learning took place? What instructional methods should be used to try to teach an "understanding"? In like manner, what instructional materials should be used? Although subject matter (for some teachers) is easily defined and well-organized, will the presentation of this material "get at" the objective related to understanding, assimilation, interests, appreciations, and attitude development? To the professional teacher, this is an area of mystery. It is an area about which he desires help.

4. *Subject-matter areas.* This area, as well as the three that follow, provides the teacher with feelings of security. Nevertheless, he still recognizes a distinct need for expert help in more clearly defining subject-matter content which should be studied in the classroom. Similarly to what happens in the other areas, the teacher makes important decisions day after day regarding the subject matter which will be taught to a pupil. Again, however, some elusive factors influence the decisions, and the scientific teacher recognizes that the choice and organization of subject matter is not always a forgone conclusion based on a systematic body of knowledge. For example, a chronological approach to teaching historical knowledge may be based on the format used by the scholar. But, although this organizational pattern used by the scholar is best suited for

his purposes, it does not follow that this pattern is best suited for a teaching-learning situation. There may be other approaches to the organization of subject matter—approaches which must be considered.[11]

For ages, the teacher has used various subject-matter approaches to help students learn. Whether these approaches are called "subject matter," "broad fields," "emerging needs," or something else, the teacher, today, wants to know about them and the factors which aid him in making decisions about their use in the classroom. Expert help is necessary.

5. *Instructional materials.* Happily, expert help is provided to the teacher making decisions about instructional materials. Not only does the teacher receive help from fellow workers, staff members, and college professors of education, but he also receives further assistance from the commercial enterprises that develop and provide the instructional materials. In the printed-matter field, publishers are quick to aid a teacher in making decisions about the use of textbooks. Models, films, recordings, film strips, and sponsored materials developed commercially are often explained to encourage teacher utilization. However, there are still gaps which need examination and understanding before decisions about these instruction materials can be made.

The teacher needs to know what types of instructional materials will best accomplish certain objectives. As an educator, he must make choices between printed matter or a film, a live resource person or a closed circuit television broadcast, a chalkboard or a printed diagram. Not knowing the potential value of the instructional material to the teaching-learning situation creates an interesting problem. Obviously, decisions to use certain materials because of known value must also be related to the student and his experiential background, the instructional methods that may be used, the physical facilities, and other factors. Failure to learn more may relegate very worthwhile materials to the junk heap. Open circuit and closed

---

[11] *Strategies of Curriculum Development, Selected Writings of the late Virgil E. Herrick*, ed. James B. Macdonald, Dan W. Anderson, and Frank B. May (Columbus, Ohio: Charles E. Merrill Books, Inc., 1965); and Tom C. Venable, *Patterns in Secondary School Curriculum* (New York: Harper & Brothers, 1958).

circuit television is a case in point, and the hope is that ways and means will be discovered for thinking seriously and co-operatively about this medium and its uses before it fades away as did radio.[12] Actually, the same point could be made about textbooks. The failure to think seriously about even the most commonplace instructional materials does not lend itself to scientific thinking about instruction in the classroom. Time after time, teachers have expressed a keen interest in learning to use the chalkboard or blackboard more effectively. In this area, for example, expert help needs to come soon.[13]

6. *Instructional methods.* Closely related to materials of instruction are the methods or techniques used by teachers to create the specific activities of teaching-learning situations. There are wide gaps in the knowledge available about classroom methods. Every so often in professional education a publication such as *Focus on Change*[14] will shake loose the attitude of complacency about methods and procedures although these publications do little to cause further study of basic methods such as the lecture (reading or telling), the recitation, the small or large group teacher-led discussion, or individual laboratory activities. The teacher needs a wealth of information about the advantages and disadvantages of these methods, with what objectives they can best be used, how to prepare for their use, and something of the technique itself. Methods, like instructional materials and subject matter, are the tools of the educational trade.[15]

When the tools are used improperly, the student suffers. No doubt the reader can rapidly recall the ineffectual lecture techniques he has squirmed through, or he can recall the scheduled small group discussions which degenerated into a series of ques-

---

[12] See: *Research Needs in Education Television,* Report of Conference (Ann Arbor, Mich.: Educational Television and Radio Center, November 1, 1954).

[13] See: Marjorie East and Edgar Dale, *Display for Learning* (New York: Dryden Press, 1952).

[14] J. Lloyd Trump and Dorsey Baynham, *Focus on Change—Guide to Better Schools* (Chicago: Rand McNally and Co., 1961).

[15] *Teaching and Learning in Medical School,* ed. George E. Miller (Cambridge, Mass.: Harvard University Press, 1961). See Chapters 6–11 by Robert S. Harnack.

tions and answers. It may be more difficult for him to recall seemingly unreasonable, useless drill activity. In regard to the use of drill, as an example, there may have been a reason for it; but, if the teacher knew the reason and the child did not, this was probably not good methodology. A good teacher knows that drill, as a method, *requires* that the pupils understand the purpose of the drill activity—its purpose in relation to the larger, more comprehensive, objective.

The professional teacher, as we have said before, makes many choices in a day regarding the alternative techniques at his command. He may make as many as four or five decisions within a forty-five minute period, and the classroom methods may be changed on the spot to meet some new condition. Teachers want to know more about the basis for making such decisions because such choices cannot be left to trial-and-error procedures.

7. *Measuring devices.* A specific test is to a teacher what a stethoscope is to the internal medicine specialist. Both must rely on these instruments to provide them with data, and just as the medical doctor must know what he is listening for, so must the teacher know what he wants to measure. The doctor uses many instruments to provide physical health data, and the teacher has a wealth of measuring devices at his disposal. Pencil-paper tests (essay, true or false, completion, short answer), check lists, rating scales, observation forms, logs, diaries, written reports, and oral presentations are devices which need to be used conscientiously and effectively. To do this, the teacher needs expert help to use the old as well as the new instruments. He needs to know the advantages and disadvantages of all these instruments. He must also know the relationship of these instruments to the ongoing classroom situation.

Of course, basic to this, the teacher needs to know the relationship of these instruments to the specific instructional goals which he sets out to accomplish in the first place, and how well any specific instrument will provide him with the information which may show achievement of the goal. Using a stethoscope to determine a red blood count is as ridiculous as using a pencil-paper objective measuring device to determine a student's success in swimming. The decision to use a certain testing device depends on the teacher knowing a great deal about measuring devices; the decision to interpret the results of the device, once it is used, depends upon the teacher's knowledge about the total teaching-learning situation. To that end, expert help is constantly needed.

There are other areas which require further study and research in order to help the scientific teacher attain the professional life he seeks, but the above categories are the standouts. Some of the areas remaining to be discussed are educational philosophy and its relationship to the teaching-learning situation; the sociology of the school itself, and the relationship of that sociology to classroom teaching;[16] the cultural background and value patterns held by an individual teacher and the effect these might have on the teacher's decisions regarding the teaching situation; and the concept of leadership exhibited by the administration and the influence such concepts might have on the everyday decisions made by the teacher.

INSTRUCTIONAL LEADERSHIP

With the increased attention given to local school administration throughout the past fifty years, perhaps it seems paradoxical that we should identify instructional leadership as a felt need of teachers who are concerned with developing professional characteristics. However, teachers, curriculum workers, as well as administrators, have decried the lack among many school administrators of time and ability to serve as staff educational leaders. Today many administrators are bogged down in a morass of business matters that range from budgeting to buses, from ordering standardized tests to the utilization of data processing equipment, and from meeting with public pressure groups to counseling with an irate parent. These tasks take time away from his job as educational leader. This is not to say that administrators are not concerned about curricular

---

16 See: Willard Waller, *The Sociology of Teaching* (New York: John Wiley & Sons, Inc., 1965). This classic, although reprinted, was originally published in 1932. See also: H. Otto Dahlke, *Values, in Culture and Classroom* (New York: Harper & Row, 1958).

problems. They are, and they find their position rewarding when short spurts of time are found which can be devoted to curriculum planning activities. In the next chapter we will focus briefly on the responsibilities of the administrator as these responsibilities are related to the professional needs of the teacher.

SUMMARY

In summary, we believe that the needs of the decision-making teacher (academic freedom, time for teacher preplanning, opportunities for individual professional growth, improved communication and articulation procedures, assistance in decision-making areas, and instructional leadership) are outgrowths of a deep concern professional teachers have for the improvement of an instructional program. Also, there are needs which were not described (salary, economic security, status, and the like) because they are not directly related to the improvement of instruction. However, all these items are inextricably tangled, one to another, in such a way that few would dare to separate them—even academically.

CHAPTER FIVE

THE TEACHER—
HIS RESPONSIBILITIES

To achieve professional autonomy the teacher requires help in satisfying unmet needs. On the other hand, to achieve professional autonomy the teacher has distinct responsibilities. These responsibilities can be identified in terms of behaviors that are related to the task of curriculum planning. In this chapter attention will focus on three behaviors: (1) studying the factors found in curriculum theory, (2) planning curricular experiences with others, and (3) experimenting in the teaching-learning situations. Each of these behaviors encompasses many facets which could lead to further exploration. For example, the behavior of *communicating ideas to colleagues* is a facet encompassed by the others. This behavior is important; it could be treated separately. For our purposes, however, it is seen as a part of planning: the teacher has the responsibility to communicate ideas when he is involved in planning curricular experiences for pupils. Many similar examples would enlarge the list of behavioral responsibilities of the teacher. We have kept the list short; but, as each of the three areas above is explored, a side glance at or consideration of the related facets may enhance the brilliance of the total setting.

STUDYING CURRICULUM THEORY

To the beginning teacher, studying the separate factors that constitute curriculum theory looms as a very discouraging task. There is too much to study. The culture, human behavior, the philosophy of the "good life," the screens of selection for choosing centers of interest, instructional activities, and the subject matter itself—to mention but a few—require what must seem like unusual mental strength. Beginning students in other areas such as engineering, law, and medicine experience the same overwhelming task. Fortunately, or as a result of planning, organization, and experience, the body of knowledge which a teacher must learn and study, although it is growing at a rapid pace, can be presented and studied in such a way that the task certainly is not impossible.

The top-notch teacher today could be compared to the physician. During their pre-service study, both learn basic information and skills about the total picture of education or medicine. In like manner, they are expected to continue to study while they practice. After graduation, the scope of study is limited by the extent of specialization. For the teacher, specialization (unless he is a substitute teacher) begins immediately upon graduation. He is, for example, a primary school teacher, a biology teacher, or a physical education teacher. For many physicians, the age of specialization begins after graduation from the medical college. His residency quite often defines his field of specialization, and eventually he becomes, for example, a pediatrician, an obstretician, or a psychiatrist.

Fortunately, this specialization (for the teacher) enables the teacher to study curriculum theory about a specific set of teaching-learning situations. A case in point might be the high school English teacher. Generally, he has the responsibility to study curriculum theory. However, he studies curriculum theory in relation to the teaching of English to high school pupils. He is a specialist. His field of study is limited by his work. Specifically, his responsibility to study revolves about the specific job he holds. He has the responsibility to study the latest subject matter of the language arts for high school students. He studies the latest knowledge about human growth and development as it relates to the adolescent. He studies the culture of his society as it enables him to define the specific instructional objectives for his high school English students. He also studies the research findings about the teaching of English to high school students. Because of specialization, it is possible for him to keep abreast of the newest ideas and findings in order to maintain his professional qualities.

So, the age of specialization, which has always existed for the scholar, enables the teacher to gain professional autonomy. Nevertheless he must recognize the responsibility to study. He cannot ignore this obligation any more than the physician can ignore his obligation to update himself regarding drugs, surgical techniques, or research findings related to his area of specialization.

Many teachers will never gain professional autonomy because they do not know what factors in curriculum theory to study or because they refuse to accept certain factors for study as their immediate concern. Many high school teachers, in particular, have felt that a knowledge of the subject-matter area was all that was needed to teach. Certainly, detailed knowledge of a subject-matter area is important, for who can teach a class without subject matter. But the professional teacher is more than a discoverer and organizer of knowledge. He has the distinct responsibility to *teach* that knowledge to a group of students, and to do this he must study diligently those items in curriculum theory that pertain to his area of specialization.

COOPERATIVE PLANNING OF CURRICULAR EXPERIENCES

Inherent in the term *planning*, which was reviewed in Chapter 3, lies the concept that group endeavor requires group action, and that meaningful group action requires cooperative suggestions of ideas, a reconstruction of those ideas (if necessary), and group consensus.

Today's teacher engages in two types of planning activities.

First, he plans with others regarding the total educational program for a student or a group of students. Then, after vital decisions have been made regarding the order of learning experiences, the second step may take place: individual decision making in regard to his own classroom work. But, without the first step (the cooperative planning of curricular experiences), chaos would replace the order of the day.

The concept of cooperative planning is listed and emphasized as a responsibility of the professional teacher because such activity has not previously been stressed by public school administrators. Therefore, the practicing teacher is slow to recognize cooperative planning as a distinct responsibility. He does recognize the need for individual planning of day-to-day activities. Cooperative planning, however, as a necessity, is sometimes ignored or pushed aside. This does not reduce the teacher's obligation to plan with his fellow staff members.

If, in a teaching-learning situation, one considers the orderliness of subject matter for a large group of students, such over-all decision making can be left to committee meetings on the national or state level, the writings of textbook authors, or the dictates of a school administrator. The teacher, then, can be told what to teach and how much time he has available to complete the task. At completion, an end examination can be "administered" by the teacher (or anyone else for that matter) that will indicate which students are ready for the next parcel of knowledge usually found in the next grade level. Given these conditions, cooperative planning between staff members is not needed. Truthfully speaking, this has been the case and still is the case in many school systems. However, with the advent of the professional worker in education, which coincides with the growth of expert knowledge in the fields of psychology, teaching-learning process, instructional technology, and many of the other factors mentioned earlier, this "national committee" type of cooperative planning for the teacher is as limited as the pinhole box camera.

Today the professional worker does not want to be hidebound and straitjacketed by a dictated course of study which stresses the acquisition of certain subject-matter information by a large group of pupils. Today the teacher wants to be given credit for enough intelligence to define the teaching-learning situations for the individual students who make up the group with which he works. But orderliness of curricular experiences must still be recognized, and the professional teacher then must recognize his responsibility to communicate with others in order to establish this order of learning.

Obviously, such cooperative planning does not require the major portion of a teacher's planning time. The major portion will be devoted to individual classroom decision making. But cooperative planning does require time. This time factor cannot be ignored. A great percentage of cooperative planning will be informal and incidental. Teachers in the same building will always discuss learning at informal meetings during the school day in the cafeteria, rest rooms, and "boiler rooms," or going to and from school. However, the educator cannot depend on "incidental-accidental" cooperative planning. The communication of ideas about curriculum and the communication about conclusions of studies and observations demand systematic time blocks.

EXPERIMENTING IN THE SCHOOL

Perhaps it is redundant to say that the scientific teacher must assume responsibility for experimentation in the school setting and for accepting the conclusions of other research studies. Redundant or not, this is the third responsibility that the teacher must assume. We think it is the most difficult to assume, and therefore requires the greatest concentration. Such a task is time consuming, thought provoking, and idol destroying. To face up to a problem takes courage; to define it takes intelligence; to work it out takes time; and to accept the conclusions may develop feelings of insecurity. However, these tasks and their resultant feelings can be looked at in another way: they excite the imagination to discover the unknown possibilities in the field of education. The end result may be a better way to educate youth in order to maintain and improve the society in which we live.

Because of the vast number of publications devoted to this subject, it seems ridiculous to say that much experimentation in local schools has already been done. The Association for Supervision and Curriculum Development, to list but one organization, has publications which deal with action research and has devoted much talent and money to helping local schools improvise, develop, and carry out research programs. Still, the classroom teacher finds it difficult to accept his own responsibility in this area. Granted, he is busy teaching, has little time for anything else, and is plagued by paper work, hall duty, and the like. However, given the perfect set of extrinsic factors which provide for maximum involvement in experimentation, there would still be a distinct reluctance to accept this responsibility. We can only hazard guesses as to why. Perhaps professional education is such a new science that the concept of it as a science only touches lightly on the fringe of our conscience. Perhaps the format of educational experimentation in the past has been so shaky that the conclusions of educational experimentation are difficult to accept. Perhaps the variables in educational research are so elusive that the teacher has distinct feeling of doubt about conclusions. Perhaps, too, the scientific attitude (the reliance upon critical thinking, the hope to define and solve problems) does not hold value for the teacher because it has not been part of his pre-service and in-service training. Finally, perhaps the scientific attitude is just plain difficult to accept because of the culture itself. (A rapid perusal of other professional persons might show the same nonacceptance of the scientific attitude.) Whatever the reason, the situation exists. Teachers find it difficult to accept the conclusions of experimentation and research done by others.

Nevertheless, for curriculum planning purposes, the staff member who seeks professional autonomy must accept the responsibility to use and accept research procedures. He has no choice. The individual planning which a teacher does, as well as the cooperative planning, requires a scientific attitude. The hundreds of teaching decisions made each day by individuals and groups who want to be labeled professionals cannot be based on the dictates of habit, custom, rationalizations, emotional response, or no thinking at all.

Cooperative curriculum planning that encourages an exchange of ignorance is detrimental to the improvement of instruction and further curriculum planning. Of course, where no evidence exists, logical arguments regarding different theories will help group members and individuals make decisions which affect immediate classroom experiences. But, where evidence exists, it must be respected. Curriculum planning cannot live in an atmosphere permeated with a distrust for research findings. The teacher who holds to the old saw, "my mind's made up, don't confuse me with the facts," has failed to accept this third responsibility.

Once these responsibilities have been defined and accepted by the professional staff of teachers, there still remains another set of responsibilities to be considered. In this analysis of the classroom teacher and his striving for autonomy, the administrator and the community people, represented by the board of education, also have a role to play and have responsibilities which must be defined before the teacher can achieve professional autonomy. In the section that follows, we will consider these responsibilities.

RESPONSIBILITIES OF THE BOARD OF EDUCATION AND THE SCHOOL ADMINISTRATOR

In this analysis, the responsibilities of the board of education and the chief school administrator are easily defined and difficult to achieve. Simply stated, their responsibilities are to guarantee that the needs of the teacher will be met and that the responsibilities of the teacher will be achieved through assistance on their part. Implementation of these responsibilities, however, will require that the board and the administrator accept the concept that the classroom teacher should be a professional worker. Once there is acceptance of this concept, we think that implementation to achieve the distinct needs and responsibilities will become a reality.

In Chapter 4, the following needs of the teacher were identified:

1. Freedom to teach.
2. Time for teacher preplanning.
3. Opportunity for individual professional growth.
4. Improved communication and articulation procedures.
5. Assistance in decision-making areas.
6. Instructional leadership.

In this present chapter, the three responsibilities of the professional teacher were listed. They are, again:

1. Studying curriculum theory.
2. Cooperative planning of curricular experiences.
3. Experimenting in the school.

Meeting these needs and assisting in accomplishing these
responsibilities are tied to a recognition on the part of the
board of education and the administration that these needs
and responsibilities are important. This recognition of importance is tied to their further recognition of the importance
of curriculum-planning activities in the local school. In other
words, if the board and administrator do not recognize the
importance of planning activities, it is questionable whether
or not they will recognize the importance of teacher decision
making and the resultant needs and responsibilities of teachers. Therefore, we think it important for the board and its chief
school administrator to consider the total concept of curriculum planning and to consider the concept of the teacher as a
professional worker. Once this has been done and there is acceptance of these concepts, their necessary predisposition to
act will help meet the needs and responsibilities of the teachers
within the school system.

Now, the administrator is ready to construct the machinery
necessary to carry out his responsibilities. Now, he can spend
his time looking "at the trees." From this point on, his main
concern will be a systematic approach to the task of planning
the improvement of the instructional program by utilizing a
rapidly growing staff. There are a series of maneuvers he will

execute. Although none of these maneuvers will be undertaken with any military precision, there will be searching on his part to find the exact needs of the staff in relation to the instructional program. A problem census, or some similar activity, will provide him with a list of outstanding areas of unrest. To solve these problems and to guarantee the further solicitation of problems, various curriculum-planning structures will have to be set in operation.

To meet other needs and responsibilities, in-service activities will be sought, instructional materials will be examined, curriculum bulletins will be developed or purchased, and consultant help will be hired. The construction of this machinery and the utilization of it will take time. Over a period of time, however, there will be a realization by the faculty that the responsibilities of the board of education and the chief school administrator are being met.

SUMMARY

Teachers who react scientifically to the planning of teaching-learning situations and who enjoy the cooperation of the community people and the administrative staff exist only in the minds of those vitally interested in curriculum planning. In one respect, they are the figments of a fertile and hopeful imagination. However, hundreds of examples of professional workers exist who represent segments of the total picture presented here. For example, there are public school teachers who enjoy academic freedom while others enjoy receiving help in decision-making areas. Some systems have teachers who benefit from a wealth of consultant help, a string of in-service courses, or a multitude of instructional materials found in a curriculum laboratory. Other teachers enjoy experimenting in the classroom and have the support of the administration in seeking the answers to problems they have identified. Still others have and relish instructional leadership which encourages the teaching staff to think critically about those policies directly related to the instructional program. Many examples can be found which indicate that the professional scientific teacher has needs that are being met and has responsibilities that are being carried out. Our hope, of course, is that in the future all the factors listed in the last two chapters (plus those that are not listed) will be found within the same school setting. Then, curriculum planning and teacher decision making may become a reality.

CHAPTER SIX

THE TEACHER AND SUPPORTIVE SERVICES

No teacher plans in a human vacuum. Teachers are influenced by administrators, curriculum workers, librarians, school psychologists, social workers, guidance counselors, custodians, attendance officers, school nurses and doctors, audio-visual specialists, testing specialists, and reading and subject matter specialists. The unique behaviors of these contributing staff members obviously influence teacher decision making. Such behaviors not only reflect their distinct knowledge but also the general attitude they feel toward the teaching staff. For our purposes, their knowledges and attitudes support teachers and teaching when what they do encourages teacher decision making. A negative role, not necessarily by design, generates behaviors which prevent the teacher from planning for the improvement of instruction.

In this chapter, it is not our intent to define the special functions of each type of staff member listed above. Rather, we wish to describe a list of guidelines for personnel interested in helping teachers make more intelligent choices. Supportive staffs must be guided in their activities by an over-all philosophy, or way of thinking, which makes their every move one which helps teachers plan for the improvement of instruction. An exacting point must be made: The milieu in which teachers operate must be conducive to decision making and curriculum planning; and, obviously, this atmosphere will be influenced by the behavior of the supportive service personnel.

Also, supportive service personnel themselves make decisions. In the areas of guidance, curriculum work, or administration, for example, decisions are made by responsible people who then carry out certain behavioral patterns. Their behavioral patterns will be related to the knowledge they have about a situation. Nevertheless, their decisions must be made within an atmosphere which realizes that the teacher is an important decision maker in his own right, and their decisions must be made within an attitude that commands respect for teacher behavior which seeks a scientific base.

In this chapter, for the benefit of supportive staff members, we will discuss various guidelines which may help to develop this base and which may encourage teacher decision making. These guidelines may be classified as directional principles which might govern a series of action patterns. These guidelines are narrow in scope. They suggest courses of action, only under the umbrella of teacher decision making, for various supportive service personnel. These guidelines do not, in any way, give direction to a specific analysis which might be made for each area of work. Philosophically speaking, the guidelines in this chapter do suggest a way of thinking about the task of the teacher in the professional setting. This, in turn, may influence more specific guidelines written for separate supporting areas. Also, these guidelines are not too far removed, philosophically, from other statements prepared by other specific groups or people.[1]

1. *Decisions made by supportive personnel should encourage and aid teachers to improve instruction and plan the curriculum.* The wording of this guideline is purposely gentle. The key words are "en-

---

[1] See, for example, guideline statements in the following references: Cooperative Development of Public School Administration in New York State, *Modern Practices and Concepts of Staffing Schools* (Albany, N.Y.: CDPSA, 1956), pp. 14–19; and J. Cecil Parker, T. Bentley Edwards, and William H. Stegeman, *Curriculum in America* (New York: Thomas Y. Crowell Company, 1962), pp. 123–128. (The list of guidelines developed by Parker originally appeared in the *Fifty-sixth Yearbook* of the National Society for the Study of Education.)

courage" and "aid." These words imply that supportive service personnel could further help teachers become better decision makers merely by changing the tone, direction, or innuendo of their action patterns. Supportive staff members could accomplish this slight, but important, shift by thoughtfully realizing and sincerely recognizing that teachers are decision makers involved in making judgments about the improvement of instruction. In those instances where service personnel have never considered the teacher as a decision maker, they should now do so. Most supportive staff actions are necessary and helpful to the teacher. However, such actions could become genuinely helpful if the plight of the teacher trying to make choices for better teaching-learning situations were always in the forefront of the minds of the personnel who support the teacher in his work. On the other hand, some decisions made by supportive personnel need to be changed drastically before teachers can be aided or encouraged in their work. In most cases, however, all that is necessary is an added attitudinal twist of mind which would cause supportive personnel to be appreciative of and enthusiastic about the professional growth of the teacher.

In the field of administration and supervision, for example, the decisions made by a supervisor could be related to in-service education. Depending on where the administrator stands in terms of his attitude, he could make in-service education decisions which would only develop the individual growth of the teacher, the re-education of that teacher, but could in no way promote decision-making by that teacher. Similarly, decisions could be made about staff utilization. Decisions regarding staff utilization might in no way promote better choices by teachers. The same might be said for faculty load. Readers in secondary school English, and helping-teachers in the elementary school may or may not promote an increase in the classroom teachers' decision-making abilities or opportunities. Supervisiors, in like manner, who visit classrooms have been known, as a result of their visits, to stifle teacher decision making rather than to encourage it. In terms of this guideline, a supervisor who chooses a course of action, or an administrator who decides on a course of action, should choose those patterns which promote teacher decision making rather than to choose those patterns could interfere with teacher decision making.

Further examples of situations that require more drastic changes, can be cited using librarians and audio-visual specialists. Librarians, when asked to encourage more teachers to encourage more pupils to use the facilities, have said: "We can't have that because the books would get out of line on the shelves"; or: "The students would take the books off the shelves to look at them and then put them back in the incorrect order"; or: "If I encouraged teachers to encourage pupils to use this library, we would have more pupils fingering the books." These quotations represent situations in which librarians have indicated decisions which have been anything but helpful to teachers interested in improving an instructional program. In like manner, when teachers have asked to use a certain film, audio-visual men have said: "If you want to use this film, it will have to be ordered a semester in advance." In like manner, an administrative decision not to let the staff use a bus for a field trip is just as damaging. In pupil-personnel work, many counselors, psychologists, or social workers are not interested in helping teachers define better teaching-learning situations for students. Probably more than an ounce of logic stands behind the behaviors shown by librarians, audio-visual men, administrators, supervisors, or guidance workers; but, certainly, their actions do not honor or follow our guideline.

Finally, there are times when a decision made by service personnel may be contrary to a teacher's decision or may actually reverse a previous teacher decision. In terms of our guideline, nothing could be more undesirable. No examples are needed to illustrate this point since the action is common. No doubt many sincere reasons exist for countermanding a decision. Whatever the reason, such practices destroy adherence to our guideline and, further, destroy the authority of the teacher, authority in this case related to his professional knowledge and decision-making responsibilities. The decision which a teacher makes for purposes of instruction in his classroom is the final decision. It may not be countermanded. After the action pattern has already been completed, and if there is serious thought by other teachers and supportive staff members that the initial teacher decision should have been different, then a post-decision conference should be called by a responsible group or board of review to "make a second guess."

The countermanding of a teacher's decision about teaching-learning situations for his pupils may not be allowed. It is a serious offense against the professional responsibilities of the teacher. Such actions are diametrically opposed to our first guideline.

2. *Proper emotional and intellectual thinking by supporting personnel indicates, through behavior, that such personnel are on a "helping" basis or "consultant" basis, rather than a "higher status" basis.* In the school's present formal and informal operational structure, this second guideline is very difficult to think about let alone to accomplish. Human nature being what it is, everyone seems to need higher status. In an educational system where cooperation is a necessity, striving for higher status than that of someone else is not a helpful condition. Supportive service personnel need an attitude which predisposes them to think that their suggestions to a teacher, or a group of teachers, are not final or the last word. Their suggestions, which could conceivably help teachers to make better decisions, need adaptation by teachers in order to improve the classroom environment or the teaching-learning situations. Supportive service personnel do have knowledges and skills which may be extremely helpful to teachers. They may be consultants to teachers. But, they cannot assume that a "higher status" should cause their suggestions to be adopted by the teacher. Basically, their suggestions should be adopted and adapted because the teacher recognizes the suggestions as helpful and needed to improve a teaching-learning situation.

An administrator who has knowledge of school law or finance, for example, can provide sound advice. A curriculum worker who has knowledge of curriculum theory or new instructional media can offer helpful advice. A school psychologist can provide needed information about a pupil's behavioral motives. These bits and pieces about management, instruction, and learners are used by the teacher to make intelligent decisions. In other words, the professional teacher already seeks this information. He recognizes the assistance of consultant help. He does not have to be falsely impressed by a "higher status" attitude.

Perhaps this "higher status" attitude or behavior is illogical and unreasonable. Whatever the reason for its existence, it is basically detrimental if it leads the consultant providing the information or suggestions to always expect adoption or use of his ideas. Blanket adoption of suggestions is impossible since the consultant does not have the responsibility or the ability to define basic tasks in the classroom. Supervisors, for example, may not know the specific decisions which a teacher has made prior to his visit. Nor will the supervisor have a clear grasp of decisions which may be made by the teacher in the weeks to come. Teacher decision making is a continuous, on-going process which requires hundreds of minute operational decisions intermingled with hundreds of preplanning decisions made over a period of weeks regarding a specific unit of instruction. Such complex activity requires the full capacities of both the teacher's knowledge of the teaching-learning situation and his knowledge of the progress of the learner or learners at every step of the way. Series of moves are carefully planned in advance, and many complicated decisions to change are made because of immediate situations. The complexity of the planned, classroom learning environment is understood by the person immediately in charge—the teacher. Similar knowledge of the same situation by consultants is unreasonable to expect. Their suggestions, if adopted without careful modification by the teacher, may make an entire sequence of learning experiences quite illogical. This point must be understood by supportive service personnel. There help is needed, but their ideas cannot be adopted without analysis.

"Shoemaker, stick to your last." If this rule were followed, perhaps there would be no need for our second guideline. Actually, the various supportive service personnel, as well as the teachers, do have a specific, well-defined role to play in a school. Each knows his area. To quote Ralph Waldo Emerson: "All are needed by each one; nothing is fair or good alone."[2] However, higher salary schedules for supportive service per-

---

[2] Ralph Waldo Emerson, *Each and All* (1834?).

sonnel (which will be discussed in the next section), and feelings of superiority probably based on the acquisition of new and important professional knowledge, tend to make supportive personnel assume that, since they were once teachers, they may still make suggestions which are immediately applicable to someone else's teaching-learning situation. This is a natural condition, but it creates problems which constrict the role the teacher must play. Teachers have the same problem to face as they work with pupils in the classroom. The pupils have to do the learning. A pupil learns in his own way. Basically, the pupil will adapt and reorganize his own experiences in his own way.

When supporting staff members exhibit "superior" attitudes, this condition may create in teachers feelings of inferiority. Within the decision maker, this feeling may destroy his effectiveness. Certainly the teacher needs the "courage of his convictions." In the end, the supportive staff member must act as though he has valuable knowledge for the teacher, and the teacher must act as though he has the intelligence and skill to use or modify that knowledge to create his own decisions.

How can we ever reach this point? Probably, many small action patterns have to be initiated. Perhaps then the large action patterns can be changed. In other words, perhaps consideration, based on the realization that each staff member in the school has a distinct and important role to play, must be given to small items such as tone of voice, terseness of written messages, and better furniture in certain offices. When changes in such comparatively minor areas occur as a result of understanding the teachers' role and respecting that role, then the larger changes will be made. Something akin to the continuing contract system will replace tenure; rating of teachers will truly become what it is: a useless appendage; and a teacher's schedule will be fashioned by the teacher in terms of his definition of his work load.

In public education, our second guideline is already being followed in many school districts by many staff members. The education profession cannot help but move in this direction. Eventually we will reach the point where there is no "higher status" in terms of job classification. Teachers will be recognized as professional persons. This will come about because the teacher is becoming more professional each year through education, experience, and further research in his field. Still, this guideline must be strongly advocated because there is the chance that more strict adherence to this principle by supportive service personnel may encourage more teacher decision making. Further decision making will, in turn, encourage professional growth. If this be true, then it is the responsibility of the supportive service personnel, who now command more respect and more salary than the teacher, to take the lead. They should do this in order to facilitate the over-all improvement of instruction.

3. *Teachers' salary schedules should be equivalent to or higher than the salary schedules of supportive service personnel. (Practically speaking, teachers should not feel that "promotion" is away from teaching.)* This third guideline will probably be considered unrealistic. But, follow-through on this guideline may make the difference in terms of how teachers think about the jobs they hold. Given professional competence, as defined by his profession, the teacher should know that his economic worth places him on the same salary schedule as any other worker in the field of education, if not higher.

Within the school system, the teacher does the difficult job, the most difficult job, in terms of the reason for the school's being. He teaches. Practically speaking, teachers should not feel that promotion is away from teaching any more than a brain surgeon should feel that promotion is away from brain surgery. For the welfare of education, highly skilled teachers are needed in the classroom. They should not be confronted with indications, through salary schedules, that the best positions in a school system belong to the superintendent of schools, the principal, and an assistant principal.

If the criterion for salary level is professional behavior related to the development of teaching-learning situations and pupils' learning, the teachers would have the same salary schedule as any other personnel in a school building. Over a long period of time, the use of criteria such as this will probably accomplish the goal: a high salary for teachers. Other criteria, such as responsibility, experience, and education, do not really enter into the argument. They can be set aside almost unceremoniously. In terms of the task of the school, the teachers' responsibility is the greatest. Teachers and other staff members can be matched at any time in regard to experience. The same can be said about education. In fact, many teachers have more experience and education than other staff members. In other words, when using criteria such as professional activity, responsibility, experience, and education, the teachers would probably be placed on a higher salary schedule. But, this is not the case.

Of course, one unique responsibility an administrative-supervisory staff member usually has is to recommend that teachers be hired and fired. This activity may be a reason, at least in terms of the folkways and mores of school-community life, for such personnel to command higher salaries than teachers command. However, the application of this activity, in and of itself, is irrational. The sum total of the research in this field indicates that administrators and supervisors cannot make valid judgments in this area. Yet the entire process of choosing teachers, rating teachers, and dismissing teachers continues with no foundation in fact. In terms of the concept of teacher professional activity and teacher decision making, we probably have reached the point in professional education where a supportive service person can no longer realistically determine the competencies of a teacher. Staff members, once removed from the teaching task and from making decisions about the learning environment, are no longer qualified to evaluate teachers.

Supportive personnel, in this case administrators and supervisors, do not have as realistic a concept of the task of teaching as do the teachers who are active in the role. Determining the teaching role is not the job of the supportive personnel in the first place. It is unrealistic to think that the administrator, supervisor, guidance worker, doctor, etc. could define good teaching or poor teaching. (This does not eliminate rating of teachers. If teachers want to be rated in order to improve their work, this process should be used. The use of an observation record form, acceptable to the staff, developed for a distinct purpose, and used by outside-trained observers, might help a staff solve some particular educational problems.) When one thinks about teaching, teachers may be best qualified to make decisions about their profession, and other teachers are probably best qualified to make judgments about financial reward for their co-workers.

Contrary to the gnawing belief that this third guideline is unrealistic, the opposite point of view could be elaborated with very little difficulty. In university laboratory schools and in some public and private schools, teachers of nursery, elementary, junior high, and high school grades are on pay scales equivalent to or better than the supportive personnel in the same school. These teachers are master teachers who, in most instances, have distinct responsibilities for directing pre-service students or engaging in unique research activities in the classroom. With the advent of the public school staff cooperatively engaged in pre-service activities instead of a university school staff, with the advent of the clinical team approach to teacher education,[3] with the advent of unique experimentation being accepted as part of the normal process in public school work, or with the advent of team teaching, modular scheduling, or individualization of instruction, the time may rapidly come when the monetary rewards for teaching will have to be evaluated in terms of a more rational set of criteria.

4. *Suggestions for the improvement of supportive services need to come from teachers involved in decision-making activities at the classroom level of operation.* Contemporary teachers have excellent services at their disposal. The potential for improving these services depends on teachers' suggestions to the supportive staff. However, even teachers moving to the growing edge of professionalism are slow to take the initiative to do this, and supportive staffs have not encouraged teachers to speak. An undercurrent of teacher grumbling and dissatisfaction may indicate that the services are good but need to be improved and that the supportive staffs, left to their own initiative, may have wandered from the primary purpose of the school.

---

[3] Charles R. Fall, *The Maryvale Project* (Buffalo: State University of New York at Buffalo, 1966).

Professional growth of teachers and the concomitant forcible growth of teacher decision making demands more help for the teacher from the supportive staff. A teacher can rapidly become inoperative or handcuffed by a lack of instructional leadership, psychological services, visual aids, library materials, and the like. The teacher needs and uses these services more and more as he has the freedom and the experience to make choices. Without service, he cannot choose; he cannot exercise his decision-making ability. Again we have the "each and all" concept. It might be safe to say that the growth of supportive service activity is directly related to the professional growth of teachers and to the development of teaching-learning situations that are more scientific.

Supportive service staffs have not been dragging their feet. They have been exceptionally active trying to be helpful— perhaps sometimes beyond the call of duty. Administrators have sought an improved theory and practice of instructional leadership. Pupil personnel service staffs have gathered vital information about pupils. Audio-visual people have excelled at the development of media which surpass the printed page, and curriculum workers have painstakingly built a theoretical basis for identifying goals, scope and sequences, centers of interest, and specific teaching-learning situations. But, where the work of these staff members has not been related to decision making by teachers, there is grave doubt as to the usefulness of the activity of supportive staff personnel. Some situations exist where, instead of supporting the interests, needs, desires, and wants of teachers, the supportive staff has become restless and has evolved services which are not necessary or not related to the task of the school.

Many examples can be cited: The administrator who provides unneeded "in-service education" for his teaching staff may be providing a service which is unrelated to the task of the school. The curriculum worker who identifies a "curriculum planning project" concerned with the identification of the over-all objectives of that school may be developing plans which are useless and insulting to a professional staff. Many other examples could be given, but perhaps they are too obvious. Contrary to the above examples, teachers can suggest interests which are related to their individual professional growth. They can identify in-service education.[4] In like manner, teachers can and have identified curriculum problems which need solution and which take precedence over a redefinition of the philosophical task of the school. Teachers can make suggestions to supportive service personnel in order to improve these services and to make these services relate to teacher decision-making.

Because teachers have moved in one direction and some staff members have moved in another direction, a schism has caused unique problems. Teachers are not "speaking" to supportive staff members, and the supportive staff member "couldn't care less" about the teacher's task. Each seems to go his merry way destroying the basic task of the school. Whatever the cause of this schism, whoever may be at fault, the supportive staff member must take the responsibility for making our fourth guideline work. The teacher, no matter what professional sin he has committed, still commands the basic task. His is the responsibility to educate the learner. He requires the help of the supportive personnel. He is the leading actor in this production. All others will play their roles in order that he may get "on with the show." This point of view may be difficult to accept, but that is what education is all about. In reality, the pupil himself is the main player; and the teacher must make choices which will help the pupil to learn. In other words, choices or decisions made by a teacher which are unrealistic or unrelated to the learning needs of the pupil are useless for learning. As much as the teacher may enjoy and advocate a certain learning environment, he must change if a new environment relates better to the characteristics of the learner. In any case, supportive personnel need to recognize their task for what it is: a service to the development of teach-

---

[4] In the Milwaukee Public Schools, thousands of teachers have suggested and taken professional advancement programs. In 1950, the Board of School Directors of the Milwaukee Public Schools began this ambitious program, which still continues. The *Catalog of In-Service Training Opportunities,* published each fall and spring, besides listing scheduled university courses, lists short-term classes, workshops, and other opportunities "which relate to particular areas of the administrative and instructional programs in the city's schools."

ing-learning situations. If that service is improved, let the suggestions for improvement come from the teaching staff.

A situation often arises in which a teaching staff is not articulate about the needs they feel for supportive services. In such situations, other staff members who support the teacher may be helpful by identifying the needs the teacher feels but cannot express. This type of improved communication will probably result from the development of machinery which promotes communication and coordination.

5. *Communication and coordination lines between supportive personnel and teachers need to be operative in order to facilitate decision making by the teacher. And 6. Instructional problems which result from limited supportive service operations need to be defined and given high priority for solution. This activity is a cooperative venture.* System-wide curriculum-planning councils or school-wide curriculum-planning steering committees serve useful functions. Members of these groups, who are selected to represent all facets of instructional services and functions, can identify and solve most instructional situations which prohibit smooth curricular operations on the grade level, departmental level, or individual level. Beyond solving instructional problems, or recommending new courses of action to improve education, such over-all curriculum groups can also coordinate diverse activities within a school system. They can also improve communication between individuals and diverse groups.

School staffs should consider such machinery advantageous. It is not often that school teachers have the opportunity to talk on a face to face basis with other staff members about educational problems in a systematic way. In the ideal situation, the teachers talk with guidance workers; supervisors talk with teachers; and so forth, about honest educational problems and needs. Without such machinery, problems are typically relegated to useless and frustrating grumbling sessions which allow for the overflow of powerful emotional feelings which are definitely not "recollected in tranquility."

A system-wide or school-wide concern for satisfying our fifth and sixth guidelines has to be systematic, but it does not have to take form of well-organized machinery such as a curriculum council, steering committee, advisory council, or the like. The guidelines, themselves, suggest communication, co-ordination, and an attack on instructional problems which may grow out of poor supportive services or out of a lack of communication and coordination. (These may actually be one and the same.) The guidelines do not advocate the establishment of curriculum-planning machinery although this may be necessary in larger school systems. If a sacred, primary, person-to-person relationship exists, the need for the more formal, secular, secondary type of organization is neither necessary nor desirable. Such formal machinery may destroy the easy, primary relationship. However, in a larger school system, primary relationships do not exist. The larger geographical areas do not facilitate a "nose to nose" discussion of instructional affairs. The establishment of curriculum-planning machinery may promote discussion and may even encourage new primary relationships among staff members who have been separated in the past. These people, meeting together on common problems, may discover that they share the same goals, have not understood the work of the other person, and can easily solve long-standing problems.

Persons who have worked on over-all curriculum committees, where all staffs are represented, will realize that committee machinery, alone, will not satisfy our fifth and sixth guidelines. The machinery needs members who are conscientious, professional people. Scholarly people, bent on reflective thinking about instructional problems, must represent the total staff. A leadership philosophy must encourage study in depth, evaluation, problem solving, and readjustment of tentative plans for action. In other words, scientific people, who have firm philosophical convictions about these matters, make the difference. Planning, to these people, is professional and artistic.

Teachers whose professional choices have been limited as a result of poor coordination and communication between themselves and the supporting service staffs recognize the need for systematic curriculum planning on a face-to-face basis. However, when such machinery is set in motion, but the intent to use it is missing, teacher cynicism develops rapidly. Such hypocritical curriculum-planning machinery insults the teaching staff. Teachers, concerned with the improvement of instruction, need and depend on educational leaders who encourage the development of systematic organization to solve the instructional problems and who provide for improved communication and coordination among all staff members. Incidental or casual attempts to tie educators together, false starts, or trial and error procedures, rapidly jolt all staff members back to their own separate and uncoordinated responsibilities. Machinery, along with philosophical attention to our fifth and sixth guidelines, may bring the diverse groups together, may help in the attacking of the instructional problems, and may prevent the currently existing dichotomy.

Improved teacher decision making for improved learning is the goal. Teaching-learning situations for a pupil are defined when the individual teacher makes choices regarding what is best for that pupil. The decisions which the individual teacher makes will be related to, and dependent on, choices or decisions that others in the school or in the total system have made. Individual teacher decision-making possibilities will be narrowed or widened by the types of cooperative and coordinated decisions or choices made by staffs on the grade, departmental, school unit, system-wide, and regional levels—the latter represented by the district, county, or state educational system. In like manner, the individual teacher decision-making possibilities will be narrowed or widened on all of these levels by the amount of cooperative and coordinated interplay of the supportive service personnel who work for the local school system or for the regional group. In professional education, therefore, systematic curriculum planning on all levels, with all staff personnel, is a necessity. Where such planning does not exist, teacher decision making will be constricted. Instructional problems of which solutions are beyond the scope or powers of the individual teacher will further restrict the number of alternatives from which the teacher may choose. Restriction and constriction of a teacher's choices will destroy his opportunities to be professional and to practice his profession. He cannot, under those conditions, be a scientific worker.

7. *Supportive services' research studies need to grow from, or be significantly related to, the teacher's need for help.* The purpose of the

school is to help children learn in terms of the objectives stated by society. Therefore, the task of the teacher is very important. His decision making, in like manner, becomes crucial; and the research studies of the supportive service areas are significant, in one respect, if they relate to teacher decision making and the basic concepts of education. This guideline suggests that, in many instances in the past, the significance of the studies of the supportive services was not related to the teacher's job. Perhaps a turnabout is needed. Research appropriate only to the tasks of the supportive services may be insignificant to the teacher, but obviously not unworthy of exploration. Service staffs must continue to explore research areas which are related to their own special interests and needs. Still, improvement of education, generally, requires research related to teachers' needs.

In the past, if significant research studies have not evolved from teachers' needs and interests, nobody was to blame. Naturally, if the nonprofessional task of the teacher was to follow the edicts of national committees, college requirements, or the course of study prepared by a supervisor, any fulfillment of the needs, interests, and desires of teachers was limited. In the past, a textbook covering the syllabus for a specific grade level was written; a general daily schedule for secondary school classes was devised; a building with general classrooms holding about thirty children was built; and the pupils' characteristics were determined by group tests in order to identify homogeneous groups of thirty who could assimilate the course of study at approximately the same rate. Under the old system, the needs were different, limited, and, in some cases, unmet. Under the old system of limited decision making, the most obvious examples of teachers' unmet needs were the lack of a syllabus and related instructional materials and activities for pupils representing the extremes in ability, aptitudes, and interests. Classes for "slow learners" illustrate the point best. To this day, teachers who teach these children do not know what to teach or how to teach it, nor has anyone provided them with instructional materials. Is it any wonder that teachers do not want these classes? When teachers' decisions are limited by a traditional concept of schooling, few research needs evolve related to classroom planning, environment, instruction, and learning.

When, however, teachers do have unlimited decision-making responsibilities, needs evolve. These needs require definition and should become the basis for initiating a group of significant studies. At the present time in professional education, individualization of instruction, team teaching, nongraded concepts, and modular scheduling, all emphasize that teachers show concern for the individual pupil. "Show concern" indicates teacher decision making about an individual pupil in an independent study setting, in a small group setting, and in a large group setting. Immediately, merely within the areas just listed, a cluster of unmet needs, wants, desires, and interests evolve which deluge the supportive service personnel. The general grade level plan, with its old scope and sequence, is no longer applicable. Therefore, curriculum workers need to help teachers. Research in curriculum development had better provide data which can be translated into functional knowledge for the teacher. Pupil grade level placement is no longer applicable. Therefore, pupil personnel workers need to help teachers. Research about pupils had better provide data about individual pupils which are functionally useful to teachers. Present physical facilities are not applicable. Therefore, administrators need to help teachers. Research about physical facilities must be translated into action. These examples could be further developed until they encompassed each item developed in the preceding chapter. However, the examples emphasize the basic point: contemporary professional education requires teacher decision making, and such choosing requires help in the form of theory development, question answering, hypothesis testing, and careful analysis of data about topics related to the needs and interests generated by professional teachers at work.

We have not said that service staff members may not be allowed to work in research areas they deem significant. Such staff members have the right and responsibility to unfold and study topics related to their own unique sphere of work. Such study is necessary if it is felt necessary by the supportive personnel. However, the concept of "necessary" quite often grows out of the milieu of the profession itself. With the advent of teacher decision making, the profession of education will deem necessary many more studies related to the teachers' work.

The entire concept of "significance" is always fascinating to the researcher or to anyone who decides to explore in a systematic way. What is significant? Typically, something is significant when it has meaning, special meaning, or a form of importance to an individual or a group. When a topic is meaningful, full of meaning, it is no longer like any other sea shell on the beach. Its new meaning, or importance, causes the researcher to hold it gently, to look at it carefully, and to ponder what he knows and what he does not know about it. What he does not know leads him to explore. Perhaps the practice of teacher decision making has helped us to perceive many new sea shells which now have meaning, importance, and significance. Many of these topics have never been considered before; they were not perceived; they were not significant. Our seventh guideline encourages supportive staffs to think carefully about the significance of their research, and to look, specifically, at those topics which grow out of the practices of teacher decision-making in the local school.

One last parenthetical point: Most research is done by persons in graduate schools who can devote a major portion of their lives to this activity. People in public education do not have adequate time. However, our guideline implies a cooperative program involving pupils, teachers, supportive service personnel, and graduate school faculties. Basic and applied research are needed in professional education just as they are needed in professional medicine. Just as one cannot separate medical research from the health needs of a society, neither can one separate educational research from the educative needs of a society. The learner and the teacher (who plans for and with the learner) must benefit from a clinical team approach.

8. *The supportive services' basic research findings need to be translated into functional knowledge helpful to the decision-making teacher.* The lack of applicable research knowledge related to and helpful to the development of teaching-learning situations and teacher decision making has been detrimental to the improvement of instruction and the profession of education. In the sup-

portive service areas and in the foundation areas, research topics and findings are either esoteric or have never been translated into functional knowledge for teachers. For purposes of discussing our eighth guideline, attention will be given to the latter idea since the esoteric quality of area research will probably continue because of the unique aspects of these fields. Since teaching groups have become more professional, and since teacher decision making is commonplace, a distinct pattern exists which indicates that more research will be done on topics significantly related to teaching-learning situations, *per se*. This may lead to data related to teaching-learning situations in the classroom. But, most important, the next step will be the translation and the analysis of this data into functional knowledge for the classroom teacher. This process will lead to better decision making.

More immediate help for teachers might be provided by declaring a moratorium on new research and asking all students of research to analyze the data which already exists in order to find meaning for the improvement of instruction. For example, the amount of data related to teaching general education objectives and related to teaching core, multiple-period, or block-time classes is overwhelming; the amount (and quality) of interpretation, analysis, and synthesis of this data is illogically small. In like manner, at the present time, the amount of research on nongraded classes, team-teaching, modular scheduling, and various aspects of staff reorganization and school day scheduling is enormous. The seeming lack of coordination among these studies, or the lack of analysis and interpretation of the data which may come from these studies, may again mean that teachers stand to lose and that the pupils suffer.

Still more appropriate to our eighth guideline, basic knowledge discovered in the fields of administration, curriculum development, counseling, and the like, has not been translated into functional knowledge for the teacher. From the teachers' present stand in the classroom, consider the uselessness of various items of knowledge and what they might mean, if made useful, for decision making. Consider the uselessness of present knowledge related to choosing specific instructional objectives, centers of interest (unit topics), pertinent subject matter or content outlines, instructional materials, and techniques for the standard classroom, the large group, the small group, or the individual student. Consider, for example, a cluster of research studies which revolve about the underachiever. As a result of these studies, what does the teacher do differently in making choices? Social class background has been studied. What does this mean for decision making by the teacher? What functional knowledge helps him to decide the action patterns to follow? Other questions should be asked about studies related to pupil interests, aptitudes, and creativity, programmed instruction, theories of learning, reading levels, and (even) intelligence quotients. The functional knowledge available is very thin.

Knowledge from supporting staffs should be specific enough to help teachers decide if a chosen pattern of action will make learning more efficient, will impede learning, or will cause no significant difference. If this point in professional education cannot be attained, teachers can never reach a high level of intelligent decision making except as they can rely on a philosophical, logical, or historical approach to their instructional problems. Even the philosophical and historical research has not been exceptionally helpful in translating researchers' unique contributions into help for teachers. However, these last two areas are not represented by supportive personnel although they should be represented, at least, by curriculum workers and administrators who classify themselves as instructional leaders.

However, there is hope. Some research studies in professional education have opened new areas which might aid teachers concerned with making intelligent choices. The next step, which may make these studies specifically helpful to teachers, is a small one. Knowledge of such areas as major social functions, development tasks, curricular approaches, social class background, instructional materials, communication, and the unique characteristics of pupils have placed professional education in a scientific era. The utilization of this knowledge by teachers is the next step. Awareness of the need stated in our eighth guideline might make the difference. Awareness that the individual teacher is stymied, that a stultifying vagueness stands between him and decision making for the best course of action for an individual pupil, might help supportive service personnel move in the direction called for in this guideline. This move will make supportive staff members true consultants, or resource people, to teachers. Teachers need this help. Supporting staff members, alone, can provide it. The total professional staff seems ready to act in this area in order to improve instruction for learners.

SUMMARY

Teachers, on the one hand, and supportive staff members on the other hand, need one another as education becomes more professional. The teacher cannot plan without help from supportive service personnel. Without the professional teacher, supportive personnel have no reason for being. In other words, the more professional a teacher becomes, the more he needs the assistance of supportive staff members. The more help staff members provide, the more professional the teacher can become. But, the more professional the teacher becomes, the more supportive personnel have to advance their knowledge in order to provide new and more demanding help sought by the teacher. The basic question is: How does each group contribute to the other's welfare? Today, we think that the answer lies in the power held by the supportive service personnel. At the present stage of teacher decision making, the supportive personnel have the tremendous power to increase the capacity and quality of teacher decision making. The eight guidelines we have discussed are written to encourage supportive staff members to use their power wisely in order to help teachers to move toward that increased capacity and quality.

Employing these guidelines may cause the improvements we seek. Conversely, not following these guidelines may lead to a reduction in teacher decision making and a downgrading of the teaching profession. A failure to follow the eight guidelines could also reduce the need for supportive service personnel that is related to the professional aspects of teaching. That this last point may become a reality is a terrible condition to contemplate. Already, large groups of teachers have voiced strong beliefs that supervisors are unnecessary. Many administrators have assumed the functions of business managers. Curriculum workers and audio-visual specialists have assumed the routine duties of clerks by checking requisitions for materials or by cataloging new supplies. Many pupil-personnel workers have completely disassociated themselves from the curriculum of the school. Again, such conditions are terrifying. For professional education to grow, they must cease.

However, the mere fact that supportive services exist and are staffed emphasizes the expansion of the educational field as a profession. It also indicates the high professional level and behavioral competence of teachers. Further growth along these lines may be related to the ability of the teaching staff to make intelligent choices. If this is true, then supportive staffs can help the process by following the guidelines that we have discussed.

CHAPTER SEVEN

A FINAL WORD—VALUATION

Teachers make value judgments in order to develop the best teaching-learning situations for pupils. Such judgment making requires basic knowledge of the foundations of education, functional knowledge related to the classroom setting, and behavioral competencies necessary to use the functional knowledge once the decisions have been made. Still, it is easier to learn and to practice the role of the teacher than it is to decide what that role should be. The first requires knowledge and skill; the second requires the ability to diagnose. Diagnosis requires that the teacher have a scientific determination to follow a certain action pattern. Diagnosis requires that the teacher use all of the knowledge at his disposal in order to make value judgments related to goals, the means to get there, and the format of the end pattern.

These activities constitute a professional burden, a serious burden for a teacher. This should be his reason for working in the profession. He should want to make decisions for the benefit of pupil learning. Such activities cannot be shunned. Nor can such activities be relegated to someone else who is not in the classroom with a specific set of pupils. No one but the teacher can assume the task.

DECISION MAKING MUST NOT BE DESTROYED

The task is valuing. The task is making choices. The philosophy basic to the improvement of instruction requires involvement in choosing, in making value judgments; the basic philosophy emphasizes a process called decision making. The staff must advocate the process, and the individual teacher must respect and know how to use the process. The decisions made must enhance the process itself. To the teacher decision maker, action patterns chosen for instruction must allow for further decision making by the teacher and the pupil. Action patterns that tend to destroy the possibilities for further and better decision making must be reconsidered, changed, or abandoned. Obviously, the same idea holds for cooperative staff action. This is why Krug has pointed out that pupil-teacher planning is more than a technique to be used in the classroom.[1] It is, instead, a guiding philosophy. The same may be said about staff planning and decision making. It is not a mere technique for finding a course of action. It is, instead, a guiding philosophy. A staff, therefore, must not adopt decisions which limit or destroy the capabilities of the staff to do further decision making. This has been a basic point throughout these pages.

How can destruction of decision making be prevented? How can a professional staff, or an individual teacher, assure the continuous aspects of decision making? Perhaps the answer is quite simple. Assurance of maintaining and promoting teacher decision making relys on the ability of the staff to know whether or not any step in the process may be detrimental to the process, itself. To know this, individuals need to think sincerely about the process of decision making, believe in the process, and practice the activity. Then, any judgments made by a staff, or an individual, which nullify thinking about the process, believing in the process, or practicing the process must be reconsidered, restructured, or dropped since the judgment may act to stop further decision making.

This book begins with the thought that teachers can be decision makers, and many teachers are. John Dewey was quoted because he believed that teachers can be decision makers and because he strongly believed in decision making, it-

---

[1] Edward A. Krug, *Curriculum Planning* (New York: Harper, 1957), pp. 184–88.

self.[2] In order to foster that process, he, and a staff, outlined the basic educational questions and problems which needed to be thought through by the staff. Again, the emphasis is on the decision-making process. In the latter section of Chapter 2, we listed further questions or problems which are prevelant in contemporary education and which must be considered by school staffs. These questions and problems were listed because past decisions made in these areas (or one might say past action patterns taken in regard to these areas) have been stiflingly detrimental to the furtherance of the teacher decision-making process. Any action pattern, any means, or any basic ideal a staff identifies which stands in the way of further choosing is "bad." Therefore, all questions and problems related to professional education must be re-examined in order to identify ideals, means, and ends which are related to the continuance of the decision-making process itself.

The remaining chapters in this book, in order to improve the ability of teachers to determine instructional goals as well as means to achieve these goals, have suggested ways and means to further the process of group and individual decision making. Every step of the way toward achievement of instructional goals, however, is also marked with guideposts which say to the teaching staff—reconsider, reappraise, and think of the means-ends criterion before you make a final judgment. The same warning is given to the total staff: Do not decide or define any action pattern which may hamper or destroy the decision-making ability of any staff member, the learner, or laymen. The destruction of decision-making ability means the destruction of the usefulness of professional training, understanding, and believing in the decision-making process. In a school, a professional staff member who is hampered in planning is inefficient. In a democracy, however, each professional person, as well as each layman, must recognize his role and limit or modify his decision making in such a way as to protect the decision-making rights of other people. If a school staff, for example, decides to accomplish their proclaimed set

---

[2] John Dewey, *Theory of Valuation* (Chicago: The University of Chicago Press, 1939).

of educational goals, they destroy the rights and responsibilities of laymen to identify the goals of public education. In like manner, if the nonprofessional citizen prys into the mechanics of teaching and thereby makes "threatening gestures" toward a teacher, he is out of his realm, and he hampers the decision-making responsibilities and rights of the teacher.

Without destroying the decision-making process itself, professional education, on the public school level, cannot tolerate courses of action which reduce, constrict, or destroy the decision-making process of anyone involved in the process. This holds for pupils, teachers, supportive service personnel, and laymen. Or, perhaps the reverse should be stated. Professional education, on the public school level, requires that the process of decision making be practiced by all: pupils, teachers, supportive service personnel, and laymen. To the extent that any one of these groups is restricted, or that individuals within these groups are restricted, the course of action needs readjustment. Also, when this happens, not only does the course of action need appraisal, but the means used to arrive at this course of action also needs careful examination; and, in like manner, the basic ideals themselves which have led to the adoption of the means and the final course of action must be reviewed.

READJUSTMENT OF IDEALS

As human beings we tend to be impatient after we have identified a goal or ideal to be accomplished. Once the goal has been decided, we tend to seek any means, posthaste, to arrive at the goal. If such impatience to attain a specified aim leads to a restriction of planning by others, perhaps the basic aim needs re-examination and modification. Special attention should be given to this point because, in professional education, this lesson is difficult to learn. From time to time laymen have identified tasks or purposes, some of which are impossible to accomplish in public education because the staff is neither sufficiently knowledgeable nor sufficiently well-equipped. The goals are not realistic. The staff, eager to follow the dictates of the public, rather than to feel the public's wrath, tries to accomplish the goals knowing full well that had further decision making taken place on the teacher level, the goals would have been completely modified because of the teachers' realization that the staff was not qualified to handle the goal. The entire Life Adjustment program of the 1940's, or certain aspects of core programs that emphasized the problems approach or the needs approach, are typical examples of this. Many of these programs failed because the teachers were not qualified to handle these areas. Teachers, typically trained in the subject-matter areas, were hard-pressed to make decisions related to societal problems and to personal adjustment problems of youth. In like manner, the lack of instructional materials, in textbooks alone, indicated to the teacher the hopelessness of the approach. Obviously, some basic goal decisions made by laymen have to be modified.

We are not advocating that life-adjustment education and advanced concepts of core should not have been identified as goals for the secondary school. We are saying that sometimes a goal needs to be modified in order for the next echelon of decision makers to continue to practice their right of decision making. The need to readjust the goal is imperative when the means used to accomplish the goal may lead to a destruction of the process of choosing and of weighing the pros and cons before a specific decision is made. Quite often a sudden movement in education, or an innovation advocated by national committees, laymen, administrators, or teachers, is forced on an unsuspecting or nonprofessional teaching staff. Steady pressure is exerted in order to accomplish the task. Administrative staff impatience is evident. When this happens, teachers are not given the opportunity to react to the purpose of the program; they are not given the opportunity to spell out, slowly and painfully, the aspects of teaching-learning situations—the limiting aspects or the facilitating aspects—which may lead to a modification of the immediate goal but which, in the long run, lead to the accomplishment of a modified goal and the eventual attainment of the original goal.

Many a wonderful innovation, or series of general objectives in public education, have been lost because of the lack of teacher involvement—not in goal setting but in goal modification related to the teachers' realistic understanding of the limits of their decision-making abilities. Now, as the profession grows and as the teacher's decision-making ability grows, we are accomplishing more difficult programs and objectives. Nevertheless, the decision-making process must be guarded and encouraged. It cannot be protected when ideals are not realistic within the realm of teacher decision making. We must have a process whereby ideals can be modified to fit the decision-making process. Otherwise we may be going backward to a witch-doctor concept applied to modern professional education.

THE NEED IN TEACHING FOR VITALITY AND INVOLVEMENT

The teacher who decides not to make choices from the alternatives at his disposal in a teaching-learning situation is, in reality, making a decision. Such a teacher's decision allows and forces someone else to determine the professional aspects of the teacher's work. This decision cancels his option for further decision making. Such conduct seems unacceptable, unreal, and immoral because of the contemporary sophistication of professional education. The choice not to make further choices destroys the process, or the means, whereby the original decision was made. Therefore, the decision to make no further judgments must be set aside or modified. The end-in-view is not acceptable since it destroys the means whereby the end-in-view was determined.

If today's teacher has come to a conclusion, upon entering the profession, that education is a commitment of his life, then he cannot choose to make no further choices. Nor, in like manner, can a board of education, or a school administrator, ask a teacher who has made this commitment of his life to shy away from practicing a professional task. If a person commits himself to the teaching profession, this is a commitment to work, live, think, and act professionally. This is a commitment to be professionally active and alive in a contemporary educational world which is expanding rapidly because of scientific evidence, new tools, innovative patterns, and developing theories and systems. The choice not to participate indicates no commitment of one's life and further indicates that the individual has no awareness of professional education reality, or no moral purpose for joining the profession—moral in the sense that he has certain obligations and responsibilities if he is to practice his profession.

If decision making by the teacher is a standard of professional behavior, a decision not to practice decision making is, in itself, a choice to separate oneself from teaching. Of course, the immediate point of contention might be: should "decision making" be a standard of professional behavior? Philosophically—yes! However, if we concede for a moment that a decision not to make choices is philosophically acceptable, we can then consider this point of "a standard" in terms of the vitality of the profession and the participation and involvement of teachers in the teaching-learning act.

Education is the most vital process known to man. The degree to which man practices this process separates him from the nonthinking animals. The degree to which man improves this process enables him to enrich his life and add meaning to further living. The continuance of this vital process may enable man to use his intelligence in ways undreamed of in contemporary society. The vitality of change, exploration, reconstruction, and invention in government, social processes, humanities, science, leisure, and morality embodies the basic purposes of life, living, growth, and education. That a teacher, whatever his task or role in the educational picture, should not or may not be involved in this process is highly unrealistic thinking. The professional worker has a moral responsibility to be involved in the process of living, growing, and educating if he makes a commitment to this type of work.

The profession, itself, is unique in its vitality because it, too, changes and grows each hour and each day even as life follows this same pattern. Not to be a part of this manifestation of living is unthinkable to the teacher. The teacher does not instruct children or adults who are in a social limbo. The teacher instructs students who interact daily with environments which emit sounds, sights, emotions, and the like. These students live in a real world. They bring to the teacher a powerful vitality. This vitality cannot be left at the school's threshold. Instead it is brought into the classroom, and the teacher must interact with it. The choice may be negative in that the teacher may choose to ignore a vital person's experiences from the world outside of the classroom. But a choice to ignore is a choice. A decision has been made. In like manner, the school grows as an institution of a society which has problems, needs, and interests. The teacher, as a school staff member, makes choices to teach in a society that has a character. The society could be characterized with such words as urbanized, mechanized, distrustful, dependent, and the like. Again, the teacher may choose to ignore this social world and its character. Such a choice is a decision, but a poor decision which should be modified because of the need for vitality in education.

"Good" teachers recognize the need for vitality in education. They recognize the need for involvement and staff participation. They recognize the need for decision making and planning, and they recognize those practical realities which are required to make planning work. Teachers who make the commitment to enter into and to work within the teaching profession—a basic commitment of their lives—also recognize the reality of the workaday world. They choose to employ the child's immediate, social experiences because to ignore them would be to destroy the process of education. And, these teachers choose to employ the characteristics of contemporary society because to ignore them would be to destroy the process of education. In a democracy, no worker in education may make decisions which destroy education—the degree to which man experiences, interacts, lives, thinks, imagines, reconstructs, or gains meaning for the purposes of maintaining and improving the civilization of which he is a part. In fact, in a democracy no man would dare to negate the process of growth. Instead, the professional worker in education realizes that in a democracy the teacher has the prime responsibility to facilitate the entire process of education. This facilitating of the process insists on involvement and participation. Probably the surest way to cut oneself off from the art and science of teaching is to decide not to participate or not to get involved in this vital process.

SUMMARY

Professional people, in order to grow, need to practice their profession. When professionals "practice," they use their knowledge to diagnose what is wrong in terms of a series of goals or ideals. They select a course of action which is relevant to those ideals and to the limitations of their knowledge. If a course of action cannot be reached, immediate steps are taken to identify the research problems which must be solved to find whatever knowledge is needed for reaching the goals. At the same time, the ideals, themselves, must be re-examined. It is this right to practice which enables professional people to define the needs for future professional knowledge. In education, this process of valuing, *per se,* must be philosophically protected in order that the teacher can work at his profession. Then the teacher practitioner can grow as a decision maker.